Geoffrey Pearson lives with his partner Gill in Littlehampton, West Sussex. He enjoyed a career in banking and international finance. Having worked in the City of London he then lived and worked in Hong Kong and the Middle East. He has lectured at university, banking and corporate seminars in Asia and the Middle East.

Geoff enjoys cricket and football having played both to a good club standard. He has a daughter, son and two grandchildren.

To my family of whom I am so proud, and my partner Gill.

Geoffrey Pearson

WHERE'S ME TEETH

AUSTIN MACAULEY PUBLISHERS™

LONDON • CAMBRIDGE • NEW YORK • SHARJAH

A CIP catalogue record for this title is available from the British Library.

ISBN 9781398445673 (Paperback)
ISBN 9781398445680 (ePub e-book)

www.austinmacauley.com

First Published 2022
Austin Macauley Publishers Ltd®
1 Canada Square
Canary Wharf
London
E14 5AA

The main inspiration for committing my experiences and observations of the past years into print is Samuel Peyps. He must have been a huge customer of WH Smith buying several hundreds of their diaries into which he would commit his daily thoughts. It was never conclusively decided if he favoured the 3–4 days a page variety or the A4 size of one day per page. The extent of his work would suggest he favoured the A4 version.

I would like to thank Austin Macauley Publishers for having the confidence in my work to take it to publication.

Preface

I have taken time to decide where to begin my observations on life. I felt I had a number of choices, to prevaricate, to be indecisive or to sit on the fence. By the time I had come off the fence, overcome my indecisiveness and ended prevarication and decided upon January, it occurred to me it was already March. Further thought offered several alternatives, the Chinese New Year, the Jewish New Year, the Islamic New Year. It was then it all became so obvious the only place to begin was at the beginning of the Tax Year so 6th April it is and here we go…

I am married to Hazel. She has health issues and uses a battery-powered scooter to get around when outdoors. We live on the South Coast having retired and moved down from Surrey a couple of years ago. Hazel sees me as a cross between Alf Garnett and Victor Meldrew. Strangely, I can't see the similarity. Things happen to me; circumstances and events contrive to test my goodwill towards man. The following chronicle is a sample of those events. Those events themselves are 95–100% authentic but taking just a little literary licence. Names have been changed to protect the stupid.

6th April

The beginning of another year, another day.

Got up, shaved, cleaned my teeth and washed my bits and pieces. Made breakfast, coffee, cereal and toast and ate it while doing a Sudoku puzzle. Breakfast over, bits and pieces washed (socks, underwear, pyjamas, etc.) I put them in the tumble dryer for 40 minutes.

7th April

Our dog, Max was much loved. He had for some time displayed some rather unusual traits. He seldom settled down, even at night he would roam around as if looking for something. Whatever we did to calm him down didn't seem to resolve his issues. We took him to our vet, who, in turn, sent us to a special dog neurologist and she, in turn, to a dog behaviourist. The bottom line is we have been given a tape to play for him consisting of various calming sounds, and he has been prescribed Prozac.

The vet could prescribe Prozac but could not dispense it. We have to go to a local pharmacy to collect the tablets. Today was the first time I collected the prescription from the vet and walked across the road to the local chemist and delivered the prescription. As always it takes 5–10 minutes sometimes more for the prescription to be filled. Not a problem, not an issue. Eventually, the young front of house sales assistant came with a packet and asked if my name was Max? The conversation went something like this…

"No, Max is my dog. If you look at the prescription it is from the vet across the road, prescribing Prozac for my dog

Max. I am Max's owner, and I am collecting the tablets on his behalf."

"Oh, okay, yeah, whatever."

I opened the packet took out the box of pills and read the label. Everything looked reasonable, Prozac for Max. And then I read the following caveat: 'Not to be taken while driving or using heavy machinery.'

"Excuse me, miss? Can you explain this to me?" I showed her the label and politely asked.

"As my dog is not allowed to drive while on these tablets, can you ask the pharmacist if he can continue to ride his bike?" I swear to you she took the packet from me and went behind the counter to speak to the pharmacist. I will give the pharmacist her due she came out from her work station and had a twinkle in her eye. She explained that it was a 'legal' requirement when dispensing certain drugs that such a caveat should be displayed on the box label. When I pointed out once more that Max was a dog, she said words to the effect that computers produce standard issue labels and were not designed to think for themselves.

I left the shop thinking I would amuse myself many times more over the coming months as each repeat prescription is filled.

11ᵗʰ April

I love this time of year. When in the garden, or walking along the street, one can feel the first real warmth from the sun. The trees are covered in blossom, some bulbs are out, birds are singing. The high-pitched buzz of a strimmer, the sound of a mower and best of all the smell of freshly mown dog shit having lain covered for six months in the long grass.

12ᵗʰ April

Mum is staying with us for a few days. She is 95 and has early signs of dementia. Not bad enough to be 'put away', (doesn't that sound bad?) in a nursing home. But she has short term memory loss, is often confused by events and is paranoid about money and possessions. Every few minutes, she asks if we have her purse, have we got her bag? I am assured this is quite usual for dementia sufferers, and it will get worse! We were sitting in the lounge watching TV; Max is underneath the glass topped coffee table. We are sharing a packet of Wurthers Originals toffees. Round, gold foil covered toffees. Two or three sweets each into the packet, unknown to Hazel and me, Mum took out her false teeth and put them on the glass coffee table. The toffee was sticking to her dentures, and it was uncomfortable for her. Time passed, ready for bed.

"Where's me teeth?" screamed Mum. Hazel and I were oblivious to any problem. Mum opened her mouth and to be sure, no teeth.

"You stolen me teeth," Mum screamed at us.

Disturbed by the sudden shouting, Max emerged from under the table to see what was going on. In his mouth were Mum's false teeth. He had been sucking away at the toffee stuck on her dentures for ages. Despite her age, Mum swooped down and grabbed her teeth and quick as a flash slammed them back into her mouth. In the circumstances, Hazel and I said nothing. We exchanged glances knowing there was nothing really to say.

We slept little last night, giggles developing into howls of laughter.

14th April

Our son, his wife and our two grandchildren came today just for a visit and to see Mum. She dotes on them of course. They brought their dog Bow with them. Bow and Max get on well.

I don't do much cooking, that's Hazel's department, but she asked me to make a jelly to have at teatime. The kids have an aquarium at home, and I thought I would attempt a jelly in the style of an aquarium. I used a baking dish, a large one about an inch and half deep and 8" x 5". I used a lemon jelly and a lime jelly. I mixed up the little cubes with boiling water and poured it into the baking dish. I thought to add visual reality to the aquarium I would add some fish. I opened a small tin of sardines, put four into the baking dish and put the tray to set in the fridge.

Not a success.

Talking as a family about happy times and we speak of my father. He died about 25 years ago, but we still talk about him and miss him dearly. One famous story was after dinner probably on a Sunday. Dad was at the sink cleaning some pots and pans. After a good and heavy meal, he would always unbuckle his belt and undo the top button of his trousers, giving his tummy room to expand! At that time, we had a Siamese cat. For some reason, the cat pawed at Dad's leg, snagged a claw in the fabric of Dad's trousers, oops, there was Dad at the sink, trousers around his ankles standing in his briefs.

Another story that always brought a tear to our eye and certainly to Dad's was the time he confused Deep Heat rub for haemorrhoid cream. No need to elaborate!

15th April

Been raining and high winds for a few days now and notice the hall ceiling leaking water. Flat roof. Couple of saucepans. Look in local magazine for Mr Fix It.

18th April

Mr Fix It came today. Looked at the leaky problem said the flashing had come away from the wall at the side of the house. Seemed reasonable diagnosis, fair quote to start in a couple of days.

20th April

Mr Fix It arrived this morning, sorted out the flashing, sealed where things should be sealed and prepared the hall wall to decorate. One hall wall decorated. Money passes hands and Mr Fix It departs.

21st April

Damp patch appears on re-painted wall. Telephone Mr Fix It. No answer, leave message.

22nd April

No news from Mr Fix It, ring again, no answer, leave another quite expansive and specific message.

23rd April

It is now a couple of weeks since we were at the vet with Max, and we had been asked to return in a fortnight with a urine sample. Max was a spaniel. Short legs, low to the ground. He may have had a neurological problem, but there was nothing slow or unusual about his doggy habits when in the garden or out on walks. Dogs are not like humans insofar as they spray out urine to mark their territory as well as urinating for the sake of urinating. Following a dog around with a sanitised bottle the size of a meat paste jar is such fun! Is he going to? Is he going to? Bugger, missed it. Is he going to, etc., etc. When they spray to mark it often is just that, a splash and jog on…I needed to get inside the mind of this dog to try and judge when a specific bladder evacuation was a 'gotta go to wee' pee or if he were just in a splash and mark mode. If you have ever taken a dog for a walk, especially in the woods or park, you know they lead you follow. I decided upon a cunning plan with which Baldrick himself would have been pleased. I decided to get in front of Max and study him closely, look at his face. If he had a purposeful and stern look on his face, it was going to be a spray and mark, take it out of that, I've been here sort of pee. If he had a happy smile, it would be a smile of relief, a happy evacuation. Wrong. No sample retrieved.

Mr Fix IT returns my call and will come around tomorrow.

24th April

In the garden with Max, no sterile jar but a small plastic spade. (Kiddies' bucket and spade type spade) I crawl around the lawn on my knees. Another cunning plan. I found that by standing close to Max and trying to judge when he is about to pee and then swooping down beside him to try and jamb his doggy bits into a jar caused him to become suspicious of my every movement. Aside from his neurological issues, this dog is quite smart. So, the idea is to keep as low a profile as possible, crawl around the lawn with Max and when he goes to pee put the spade underneath him and catch what can be caught. Done it, Yes. No, bugger, as he finishes and puts his leg down it knocks the spade from my hand. Spade on floor, dog 20 feet away, hand drenched in urine, trouser knees green and muddy, wife hysterical. Me? Can't quite see the funny side; maybe later?

Mr Fix It is bemused that damp patch should appear on the wall. Suggests taking off the plaster back to brickwork, sealing and starting again. No more leaks so roof repair thankfully holding.

25th April

In the garden with Max, plastic spade wearing shorts and a pair of marigolds. Now getting the hang of this. Creep up behind Max, when he cocks his leg, slip the spade under him, don't be greedy on the amount received, withdraw spade slowly with a firm grip and hope he is on bladder evacuation mode and not spray and mark. This being his own garden my thoughts were he would be on bladder evacuation mode rather than spray and mark. I think I am right as after about four attempts I have a decantable amount in the spade to pour into the sterile bottle. Done it, off to the vet.

Got to the vet after lunch and found a new receptionist at the desk. This is not unusual; they have quite a high turnover of girls, probably on work experience or even trainee veterinary nurses. I am feeling mighty proud of myself, sterile jar in hand containing a meaningful amount of urine. "Mr Hamble asked for a sample of urine from my pet goldfish Max," I said to the girl.

"Fine, thank you," she said and rose to take the jar. I looked at her straight in the eyes. She looked at me, and I could see she was running over in her mind exactly what I had said to her. She started to laugh; firstly, with her eyes and then her mouth and then her brain kicked in…Suppose he is right? Suppose this is goldfish urine? I've laughed in his face; he is a customer. Oh, I wish I were dead. I hate it here. Pity then overcame me, and I told her the sample was in fact from my dog as requested by Mr Hamble. The young girl calmed down apologised where, of course, no apology was due.

"Oh, by the way," I said, "while I am here do you have any pick me up tablets for my other pet? He seems to have the right hump these days?"

"You will have to bring him in for Mr Hamble to see," she said. "What kind of pet is he?"

"A camel," I said as I went out of the door quickly.

27th April

Urine tests for Max not good. He has more medication.

I need to either resow some of the lawn with grass seed or get some turf strips. I decided to buy some ready grown turf. A sign at the garden centre said £4.29 per sq. metre. It then said the turf was in strips 24" by 64". This rather confused me so I asked the girl at checkout who was not busy to explain. She said the strips were indeed 24" by 64" in length, but if you cut the strip in half, it was a square metre. I explained to her that by cutting the strip in half you would have two strips of 24" by 32", which is still not a square metre.

"Oh," she said, "the strips are £4.29 each anyway."

"Thank you," I said, "I'll have two strips in green please."

"What do you mean?" she said.

"I don't know what range of colours you have, but I just want green," I said.

"The grass is outside in front, that's all we have."

"Okay. I'll have two of those then, they looked green to me."

28th April

Laid two strips of turf, watered them in, stamped all over them but I am really going to need another one piece to finish the job so I went back to the garden centre. Rolls of turf still outside. Different lady at the checkout. "May I have one roll of turf please in green?" I asked.

"I don't know what colour they are as they have been there since Friday. I'll let you have it at half price!"

"Thank you," I said wondering if I really heard her correctly. Looking at my change, yes, she had sold it to me at half price.

Mr Fix It came this afternoon. Hacks off plaster from an area two foot by three foot on the wall. Applies sealant to exposed brickwork and leaves.

29ᵗʰ April

Max had always liked sweets; peppermint seemed to be a favourite. This was demonstrated very graphically this morning. I found him lying with, almost on top of, Hazel's handbag. The bag was open and its contents strewn across the floor. Max saw me coming, sprung up and ran out of the room. There was something different about the way he ran. Yes, he was dragging something with him. I took a couple of moments to shuffle the scattered handbag contents back into the bag. Usual handbag contents, kitchen sink, spare wheel for the car! And also sweet wrappers, Tunes, sweet wrappers. I then went to find Max. I found him in the dining room under the table. His face told the story, very sad and ashamed. Not I feel about the sin but by being caught. How could he deny he was the thief? The bottom half of his face was pink; one Tune was sticking to an ear another attached to a front paw. The remains of the packet were stuck to his tummy. Max got up and walked towards me. You could see he felt awkward, heavily laden with sticky Tune sweets, packaging and general pink gunk. 'Busted.' 'Please clean me up.' What can you do? Laugh, shout? The answer had to be pick him up at arm's length, take him into the kitchen, sit him in the sink and wash him. My wife's cosmetic scissors helped in clipping away some of the more obstinate gunky bits. Max continued to love sweets, but we tried to be more careful where we left confectionery.

30th April

Mr Fix It re-plasters wall. Leaves.

2nd May

Went to lunch at Pizza Hut. The menu had side orders of coleslaw, chicken wings, sweetcorn and baked potato wedges. I asked the waitress for some potato wedges with my order. "Oh, yes, you mean skins," she said.

"Whatever you call them. How many in a portion?" I asked.

"Four," she replied.

"Okay, I'll have the chicken wings," I said. "If you think I am ordering a portion of foreskins, you must be joking." The meal was quite good, but I kept getting strange looks from the staff.

3rd May

Went to Hayling Island to look around. Hazel enjoys craft work, knitting and watercolour painting especially. As she has mobility problems, she uses a battery-powered scooter to get around. We went into a rather nice craft shop. Small aisles and very well stocked. Being in a tourist resort, this particular shop has lots of 3xT. Tasteful tourist tatt including rotating stands of postcards, standing in the already cramped aisles. Hazel blithely motors up and down and around the aisles; I follow picking up wool, books, tins knocked from the shelves and generally cleaning and clearing up after her. The mobility scooter does not have rear view mirrors, and she never uses her reversing beeper. Hazel had obviously finished looking at whatever had caught her attention, and as there was no way forward, she reversed. The chap standing behind her never had a chance. She reversed into him; he jumped and fell into a rotating postcard stand. The postcard stand fell into a rack of wool. The word dominoes came to mind, cause and effect, etc., etc. The rest is history.

4th May

Mr Fix It returns and paints wall. My wife by this time has christened this jerk 'wing nut'. Short, shaven head, big stand out ears.

5th May

I am amazed (really) to see a crack in the newly painted wall. The wall is perfectly dry; the ceiling does not leak anymore, and I have seen Wing-nut take the plaster off back to brickwork, seal the wall and redecorate. I am not a fan of Wing-nut, but do have sympathy for him. Phone Wing-nut, no answer, leave message.

7th May

My wife began a new therapy class today. I drove her into town, delivered her to the prescribed location and had an hour and a half to kill. I had not been around these parts before and was at a loss what to do so went into a local pub to while away the time. I was standing at the bar minding my own business and there were three chaps also at the bar standing maybe ten feet away. They were talking about their jobs, their likes and dislikes. It was quite early and the pub was empty apart from us and their conversation was easily overheard. One said he was a teacher. He loved the idea of teaching young people and could see their development over years. He did not like the growing lack of respect and discipline endemic in the school. Another was a fourth-generation fishmonger; he had grown up within the fishmonger tradition and loved it. He went sea fishing himself but found there was always a lingering fishy smell about him and his house. The third guy was an IT Programmer. He says he earned good money but was stuck indoors at a desk all day and would very much prefer to get outdoors once in a while. After a brief silence, one of them turned to me and asked what I did for a living. I was not in their company as such so I was a little taken aback by the question. I don't know what possessed me to say it, but I said I was a professor of logic at Chichester University.

"Oh, what's that all about?" asked one.

"Do you have a shed?" I asked.

"Yes," he replied.

"Then you have a garden."

"Yes."

"You have a shed in your garden, so I assume you have a house?"

"Yes."

"You have a shed in the garden of your house, you are wearing a wedding band so I assume you are married?"

"Yes, I am married with two children."

"So, you have a shed in the garden of your house, you are married with two children. May I assume you therefore have a good and active sex life?"

"Yes," he said beaming a huge smile as if I were a magician.

"So," I said, "from the knowledge that you have a shed, I can deduce purely by logic that you have a good and active sex life."

At that time, the door of the pub opened and in walked a chap obviously known to these three guys.

"Morning, John, you got a shed?" asked my new acquaintance.

"No," said John.

"Then you're a wanker," they all shouted in unison.

I drank up and left quickly to fetch the wife.

8th May

Got answerphone message from Wing-nut, we must have been out when he phoned. Phone Wing-nut, no answer, leave message.

9th May

Another month had passed, and I need another prescription for Prozac for Max.

Got the prescription from the vet but need it dispensed from a chemist so I decide not to go back to the chemist opposite the vet's but go to one further up the road. Waiting for the prescription, I wandered around the shop looking at what is on the shelves. My inner demons took over. I picked up a packet of condoms, walked up to the counter and asked,

"Do you have a fitting room I can try these on for size?"

The answer was a very firm 'No'.

The mood in the shop was such that I thought maybe I would save the Max and his bike gag until another time.

10th May

Wing-nut calls, be here tomorrow at 10.00.

11th May

Phone call from Wing-nut, cannot come due to an emergency of a client. Will phone and re-arrange visit.

Feeling a little tense. Went out for a drive to nowhere in particular and finished up at a nice pub in Emsworth, overlooking the harbour. Hazel fancied a large glass of red wine and I had an orange juice and soda.

"Do you want ice with that?" asked the barmaid.

"Is it fresh or frozen?" I replied.

"What do you mean? Is it fresh or frozen, of course, it's frozen; it's ice!"

"Okay, then leave it out," I said. "If it were freshly made today with nice fresh water made in an ice making machine, I would have had three knobs. As you say it is frozen, it could be 60 years old and kept in a freezer until now. It could have frozen insect droppings and other nasty things. It could be left over from Korea or the Vietnam War. You say it is frozen, well, not for me, thank you. I'll take my juice as it is."

As I turned with the two drinks and walked out of the bar onto the patio, I could feel her eyes digging into my back. All I asked was a simple question. Am I not entitled to fresh ice? You listen to all the cooks on the telly. They all go on about fresh produce.

12th–13th May

Max is not very well. He is not drinking, not eating, does not want to go out for a walk and is very droopy when cuddled. And I decide it is vet time again. Thank heaven for insurance.

Consultation and injection. Home we go and hope for improvement overnight.

I am not in the best of moods. Feeling very worried about Max. My friend Wing-nut called. In hindsight, perhaps I was a little harsh. Words seemed to tumble uncontrollably from my mouth. Hazel told me afterwards she thought I was a little irrational in my diatribe. By mutual consent, Wing-nut will not be returning. When I say 'mutual', I don't actually think he spoke much, but I am sure he will not be back.

Had a cuddle with Max; he is not looking good.

14th May

No improvement in Max. Back to the vet. It is mutually decided Max's time is nigh. Hazel and I are left with him in the consulting room 'for as long as we want'. I can't take more than a minute before I run out of the surgery and into the car crying my eyes out. Hazel followed two or three minutes later also crying. We drove home in silence knowing it was the right thing to do, and he would have been suffering and miserable if we had delayed the inevitable. The injection which put him to sleep was a release.

Our friends and relatives all knew of Max's problems and that he was not well. That evening, many telephoned to ask how he was. I could not speak; I just collapsed in tears every time they asked about him. Neither Hazel nor I can be bothered to cook, and we do not fancy eating out, so I went to the local chippie. Ordered two large cod and chips. As I came out of the shop holding the hot and steaming bag, I caught sight of a man sitting on the floor leaning against the chip shop wall. "Evening, mister, I've not eaten for three days."

"I admire your will power," I said getting into my car. I was thinking about the continuous diet that Hazel was on and felt if she had the same resolve, she would lose more weight.

15th May

We are as miserable as hell. We talk about Max and the good times. When he was younger, we showed him at dog shows and have a collection of many rosettes including several firsts. We remember a winter or two ago when overnight six inches of snow fell. When we opened the back patio doors for him to run out and 'do his business', he jumped down and disappeared. The snow was deeper than he was tall. I remember carrying him out to the main road where overnight gritting and early traffic had flattened the snow. There was now no traffic about; there was an eerie silence and just me and Max walking along the middle of an A road. We went to the woods where the overhanging canopy of trees and branches shielded the woodland floor from the worst of the snow. I had to carry Max home as the pavements were still too deep in snow for him to walk. Over the next couple of days when Max was able to go outdoors, he would return with ice balls stuck to his paws and tummy. We would put him in the kitchen sink to thaw out and remove the ice balls. We spoke of the time only last month, when Max pinched Mum's teeth to suck off the toffee. We spoke of many happy and fond memories, RIP Max. We loved you.

18th May

Went to the vet. I needed to settle his account and collect Max's ashes. There was another new face at reception. "Good morning, I have come to collect Max," I said. The girl went out back and soon came back with a small box.

"What's this?" I asked.

"These are Max's ashes," she said.

"I only brought him in for a shampoo, haircut and his nails trimmed."

The look on the girl's face was a mixture of grief, terror and the unmistakable signs that she was about to have a fit. She ran out back again. Moments later, the senior nurse came into reception followed by the distraught young girl. She gave me 'the look'.

"I've just come in to pay my bill and collect these," I said showing her the box.

Words were exchanged between the two ladies, which I didn't quite hear, but the gist of it was 'this chap is a lunatic, he always winds up the staff, just keep cool, get him his account and send him on his way.'

19th, 20th, 21st May

Hazel has started to feel very unwell; she now looks like Marge Simpson. Very yellow. A hasty doctor's appointment is made, and after an examination and blood taken, it is suggested she has hepatitis.

23rd May

Blood test results confirm hepatitis. Hazel does not want to eat or do anything; she is completely wiped out.

Pretty much isolated at home.

24ᵗʰ May

Crack in paintwork on hall wall has not got worse, nor has it disappeared!

I couldn't care less.

27ᵗʰ May

I am feeling lousy, listless, don't want to eat. I am yellow and pee dark brown. I too have hepatitis.

The Environmental Health people kick into action. Hepatitis is an infectious disease, and they are obviously worried as they are on the phone asking where we have been, where we have eaten, with whom we have exchanged bodily fluids! Apparently, another six cases have been diagnosed in a five-mile radius.

14ᵗʰ June

For the past fortnight or so I did not have the inclination or strength to keep my journal up to date. I went from bed to sofa to chair to a different sofa to bed in no particular order, but at all times feeling as ill as I ever felt in my life.

Let me think what has happened?

Garden untouched. I have no strength to even look at the lawn mower, and as for weeding, I hardly have the strength to pull the top off a milk bottle let alone pull out any weeds. Looking either at the local newspaper's Classified Ads or the local magazine; I contacted two or three gardeners. One went by the name of Doug; I thought, that's a good name for a gardener, so I appointed him.

I need to have blood tests. Sharp, pointed metal things and me do not get along. My phobia started when I was about 10 years old. Poliomyelitis was a major problem and school children were being vaccinated against it. At that time, this was by injection; I believe, three or maybe four injections taken over a short period of time. I fainted after each of the first three. If there were to be a fourth, I don't believe I ever took it. Over the next 50 odd years, I avoided all inoculations, TB, smallpox, tetanus at school and now the flu jab. Anything that was going, I avoided it. I even developed paranoia over going to the dentist. My earlier recollections of the dentist were that they used gas to knock you out and get on with their business. Over the years, they used numbing injections too and that was when I stopped going.

I need to go to the doctor's surgery for a blood test to monitor my hepatitis. Hazel asked if I want her to come along. I don't. I am very, very nervous and would rather face the unknown on my own. My name is called. "I am in no hurry," I say aloud. "Anyone who wants to go in please take my place." Silence. There are only a couple of people in the clinic, and apparently, they have appointments with specific doctors or are as shit scared as me.

I went into the nurse's room, and she asked me to sit in the chair by her desk. I explained to her that I was not feeling my best and could I lie down. This she allowed me to do and proceeded to suck out my blood.

To be honest, it was virtually painless. I strode out of her office chest puffed out. I was the man. It was only when I was half way home and had stopped running, it occurred to me perhaps I should have asked 'what happens next?'.

I returned rather sheepishly to the surgery and was told to come back in about 10 days for another blood test.

16th June

The lawn has been mown, strimmed, hedges cut and the garden generally looking quite good. I am still very weak and not really able to do much at all. Hazel's illness is about two weeks ahead of mine. We have been to hospital for tests on her liver but all seems to be fine, and she is beginning to feel better.

17th June

Decided today that the crack in the paintwork in the hall must be addressed.

Talked to Doug the gardener who says he will 'fix it'. There is now a lack of urgency so we agree upon 'sometime soon'.

18th June

Summer is progressing and the weather has been excellent here on the South Coast. Police in this area do say that at this time of year the crime rate rockets by about 40%. I am sure that of that increase, 99% must be dealt with by the 'Crimes against fashion' police. People who in all other circumstances must be sensible human beings, presumably holding down a job, able to vote and conceive children, wearing all manner of hideous garb. Shorts, some of which start at just above the ankles and go to up beyond knee length. The shortness of the shorts being directly proportionate to the fatness of the thighs. Guts that hang pendulously over the waistband. Bums screaming to be freed from overtight restriction. Most are wearing tops that promote a sport or a superhero. Hello! The brevity of their apparel allows otherwise unseen tattoos to emerge. Tattoos on ankles, calves, arms, necks and chests the designs and colours of which have been distorted by bodily growth, time and gravity so that what remains is similar to an explosion in a jam factory.

The men are just as bad.

19th June

My birthday was a few weeks ago but felt so ill it passed without note or celebration. I now have several pounds worth of M&S vouchers to spend and feel able to face the world. We went today to a very large M&S superstore outside Southampton. It is located on a retail park with other huge retail outlets. Wandered around the Men's Department while Hazel toured the Women's section. She has no vouchers but a huge female urge to spend money on the unnecessary and unwanted. I am sure a woman's mission in life is to see how much clobber can be crammed into a wardrobe. I digress. I select a jacket, a couple of pairs of trousers, a pair of shoes and two sweatshirts. The Men's changing room was well signposted and easy to find. This was a huge store and the changing rooms were suitably large. On approaching the changing room, I saw three signs. 'No Smoking'. Fine, understand that; smoking has not been allowed in most shops, restaurants and pubs for a number of years. 'Ask attendant for assistance'. Okay, I have been dressing and undressing myself now for many years and thought that this command that I ask a young lady to assist me in taking my trousers down may be misconstrued. There were, in fact, two young ladies in charge of the changing area. I approached them, pointed to the sign and said I was quite able to manage the function of trying on various items of clothing. They looked at me and explained the sign was not 'a command' but an invitation for customers to seek assistance if perhaps they needed another size or colour garment rather than go into the store and seek out alternative clothing. "How many items do you have, sir?" asked one pointing to the third sign. "Only five garments allowed in changing rooms at any one time." One, two, three, four, five, six. Bugger.

20th June

Doug arrives to cut the lawn and strim. Asks if it is convenient to rub down and decorate the wall in the hall. All done and sorted.

23rd June

We have a large number of books. I have taken to reading novels, mainly fiction. I read fairly quickly so the window ledges are getting rather full with books, and it is decided we need to buy some book shelves. The shelves will go in the dining room where we have dark wood furniture. We decided to look in second-hand shops and hope to find some 'old' brown wood shelves.

25th June

Now been to every charity shop and second-hand/junk shop around. Hazel remembered there is a second-hand shop about 10 miles away we pass going to visit our son. We found the shop easily, parked and I walked to the shop. I noticed the shop sign said 'Previously loved'. I thought that was a promising sign for decent second-hand furniture. I went into the shop and found I was surrounded by hundreds of garden statues, ornaments, fountains down to gnomes. "Can I help you?" asked the man behind the counter.

"Yes, but I was looking for second-hand furniture," I said.

"Oh, the chap who used to be here has passed on."

"Was it a cremation or burial?" Stony silence, mouth open. His chum doubled up with laughter.

"No, I mean he has left and gone to Yapton."

30th June

Hazel was sitting on her chair in the lounge and called to me to say something was stuck in our chimney. She could hear noises. I came into the lounge, and yes, there was a scratching sound from up in the chimney breast. I hoped it would go away. What can I do!

About half an hour later, Hazel calls again to say there is a bird in our log burner stove pecking at the glass door. Yes, there was; I could see it. Various scenarios came to mind. The most obvious was to open the stove door and let it out. The downside to that was the bird being unfamiliar with the layout of our lounge and indeed the inside of our house it would almost certainly panic and fly into walls, furniture and ceiling leaving sooty smudges everywhere. Discounted option one. Second option was to open the door slowly and for me to catch it and take the bird outside. I discounted this option immediately as I cannot stand birds. Horrible scrawny, bony things that flap. I envisaged being brave and having a large bath towel in two hands seeing if I could rescue the bird. On the basis of 'sods law' if something can go wrong, it will; I could see me opening the doors and not getting the bird secure first time and it flying around the room attacking me and bashing into walls, ergo a combination of option one and two. I made a decision to call the RSPB. They rescue birds, no problem. I tried to find their phone number in the telephone book. Do I look under T for The, R for Royal, B for birds? Couldn't find the number. Tried RSPCA. Same problem. Tried local Council Environment Department, their number was in the book. They were not interested in my trapped bird but gave me the phone number for the RSPB. Phoned RSPB, they are not interested as it is a wild bird! They told me try the RSPCA and gave me a number. I was contacted to an answering service. Press 2 for wildlife…pressed 2. Is there a wild animal in distress or trapped, press 2. Did so and moved on…If the animal is stuck up a chimney, call British Gas to disconnect the supply, all charges are for your account! No, don't want this option; it is not stuck up or behind any gas utility. I went back to the menu to try again. I confirmed that I had pressed all the correct buttons as offered for my wildlife in distress or stuck in a chimney…and I am back to being told to call British Gas. I rang off. A brilliant idea, go to the local vet; they are only a five-minute walk away. They must have people who are not paranoid about little bony, scratchy, flappy things and would not want a creature to remain in distress. I walked to the vet and explained the situation. 'Sorry, can't help', but they gave me the phone number of the local Wildlife Trust. They look after and care for wild animals. Came home and phoned the Wildlife Trust. "Sorry, can't help, there are only two of us here, and we are looking after over 200 animals." I now decided to call the local pest control company. Brilliant; they arrived within half an hour, rescued the poor tiny creature and released it in the garden. It was apparently a starling; immediately, two other birds swooped down to the released bird and obviously began a parent to child discussion about not falling down chimneys. Seconds later, a swarm of starlings flew in and they all began a cheerful reunion, hundreds of the little buggers. It cost me £50 for the pest control men but money well spent. No more scratching for the chimney. It does rather reinforce my scepticism about charities.

2ⁿᵈ July

The gardener, Doug, has told me he can no longer work for me. His gardening business has thrived so much that he has sufficient work local to where he lives; it has become uneconomic for him to travel to and from my house. I can understand this and agree with him; it makes good business sense to consolidate his work more local to where he lives. Good bloke, does a good job and is reliable. So, I am back to the local magazine and local newspaper to find another gardener.

3ʳᵈ July

During the day, I have had three gardeners look at the garden. Mowing and strimming every two weeks, cut the hedges twice a year, weeding and general maintenance (dead heading) as and when necessary. Two quoted 50% more than I was paying Doug, and another said as he was so tall he didn't do weeding! I am allowing myself some leeway and widen my search.

7ᵗʰ July

I saw a postcard in the post office window advertising gardening services. Sounds ideal I thought, gave the chap a call. He is coming over tomorrow.

8ᵗʰ July

Gardener arrives looked around the garden and gave me a price. I didn't bite his hand off immediately, as a one-armed gardener may not be as competent. He was cheap, local and willing to start immediately. Doug was here recently so the lawn really does not need mowing for another week. I told Mr Kerr to cut the hedges to start and then next week to mow and strim the lawn.

9ᵗʰ July

Mr Kerr arrived to trim the hedges. He has an electric trimmer so I showed him the power point in the garage and the 'Green' wheelie bin for garden rubbish. Hazel had a hospital appointment, so we paid for three hours' work to finish the hedges, drove off asking him to close the garage door when he was finished and 'see you next week to do the lawns'.

Arrived home, hedges trimmed, garage door wide open. Mr Kerr and his car are gone. Along the entire length of the hedge inside my garden is a line of hedge leaf clippings. Something told me to look the other side of the hedges along the pavement and public footpath. Correct. Hedge clippings for as far as the eye could see. I cleaned up using broom and skrake. I think it is called a skrake, a wide long toothed rake used for dragging leaves.

11th July

My grandsons both play football for their local club. One is eight, the other six. My son manages one team and my daughter-in-law the other. The club is quite a big club; they have their own ground, stands, bar, etc. and a lot of surrounding land. The senior men's team play in one of the top amateur leagues, and they have about 15 junior teams, both boys and girls who play on the adjacent pitches. The season has started and Hazel has decided to knit a woolly mascot for the youngest grandson's team. She is knitting an octopus.

16th July

Woolly octopus finished. We have already purchased a stiff cardboard, padded envelope in which to post the toy to our daughter-in-law. I went to the post office in town. Reasonable size, maybe six windows for service, a Bureau De Change, a separate counter where they just sell stamps, cards and odds and ends and another parcels collection unit. It is a big post office, and you would expect, no, sorry, I would expect the staff to be of at least average intelligence. Hold that thought.

There is a queue. Four of the windows are staffed and in use. I wait my turn. Eventually, a customer left one of the windows; it is my turn, and I walked to the window.

"Please return to the queue; I am going to lunch. That is why we have the announcement to 'please go to window number when the next assistant is ready to help'." I felt sheepish and returned to the queue. The next two or three in the queue showed emotions ranging from sympathy for me to smugness that it wasn't them.

"As we are busy, I'll serve you and go to lunch later," said the charming lady. I took a deep breath and walked the four paces back to the counter. I placed the envelope on the scales and asked for a first-class stamp. She told me the price, and I slid the envelope through the window.

"What is it?" she asked.

"An octopus," I replied. Her head jerked backwards; her chair noticeably wheeled backwards. She grabbed a book from beside her, flipped through it and said to her colleague, "I don't think we are allowed to take octopus, are we?"

"It is not a real octopus, you daft cow," I said. "It is a toy." I don't like swearing, especially not at ladies, but I was so incensed by this woman, words just came out. The queue, especially the first two or three who had witnessed and heard all that had gone on were in hysterics.

17th July

Mr Kerr the gardener arrived. We had a discussion as to why he had left all the hedge clippings on the ground and not cleaned up after himself. He didn't have a broom! Why did he leave the up and over garage door open? Forgot to close it! Not the best of starts, but he is cheap.

"Can I borrow your mower?" he said.

This question caught me rather by surprise. To be asked by a gardener if he could borrow my mower! I showed him my electric Flymo. Fifteen minutes later, he knocked on the door and said he was not making much progress, would I mind if he called it a day, went home and came back tomorrow with his own mower. It seemed an excellent idea to me.

18ᵗʰ July

Mr Kerr arrived with his own Flymo.

Cheap, local gardener doing a job.

I was working on the PC and Hazel knitting, watching the television. What could go wrong?

PC crashed. I went into the lounge, TV off. Walked into the kitchen and see all the red fuse indicator lights are also off. Turn on lights, no lights. I went into the garden. Mr Kerr is sitting on the grass with a piece of electric flex in each hand looking rather sad. He had mown through the cable and blown everything. "Do you have any duct tape?" he asked. "I've done this before, and I just need to tape these two ends together." I re-run that last comment in my mind, 'I've done this thing before, and I just need some tape.' It then occurred to me. Doug, my ex-gardener, wore a hard hat, goggles, ear protectors, heavy duty trousers and boots. Mr Kerr was sitting on the grass wearing flip-flops and shorts. We decided that he would not be returning, and I would again try and find a gardener.

19ᵗʰ July

I play indoor bowls twice a week, and for several weeks on two or three occasions when delivering the bowl, I have felt very giddy. Also, if I get out of bed quickly, my head swims. Due to the various issues Hazel has with her health, we have a DIY blood pressure kit at home. Hazel insisted I took my blood pressure, and it was quite high. There has been a lot of publicity recently about heart attacks and strokes. My father died of a heart related condition so I agreed to go to the doctor's surgery and get the nurse to test my blood pressure and get her opinion.

20th July

Saw the nurse and she suggested making an appointment to see the doctor as my blood pressure was quite high. At reception, I made an appointment to see a doctor next week. Soon after I got home, the telephone rang; it was the surgery. There was a cancellation and could I come back to see a doctor this afternoon. Now, was that fortuitous? Or when the nurse put her notes of my tests into the computer, alarm bells went off and I was asked to present myself back at the surgery?

Later that afternoon, I met a very nice lady doctor, new to the practice. She ran through some general health and lifestyle questions.

"Did I smoke?"

"No."

"Did I exercise regularly?"

"I play indoor bowls a couple of times a week and walk most days."

"How far do you walk?"

"Depends how far away from the pub I park the car."

"So, you drink alcohol!"

"Yes."

"How many units?"

"I think they say somewhere around 25–27 units are safe for men. Some days I do, some days I don't."

"That is a weekly maximum, not a daily target!" The doctor seemed to be getting a little stressed!

"Take your shoes off and stand on the scales, please," she said. Doing as she requested and then having my height checked, she said I needed to lose weight. She thought I may have benign positional vertigo, which is reasonably common in older people. If I lost weight, she thought my blood pressure would go down. She asked that I made an appointment to see the nurse again for blood tests, urine tests and an ECG and come back to see her in a couple of weeks.

We then spoke about my diet, and she said I had to give up salt, sugar, white bread, butter, beer, spirits, wine, fatty foods, puddings, chocolate and full fat milk.

"That just about takes away all enjoyment in life," I said. "What about sex?"

"That's fine," she said.

"Okay, I'll pick you up around 7.00," I said closing the surgery door behind me.

22nd July

I saw the nurse today for a fasting blood test, urine test and ECG. Booked in to see the doctor in a week. Obviously, my blood sample needed to be sent away to the hospital. The nurse tested my urine immediately; I said she could keep the sample; I did not want it back! She took my waist measurement, height and weight and said I needed to lose quite a few pounds and reduce my waist size. I said that as I was such a clever fellow my brain was at least ten pounds heavier than most people so she should take that into account. She said she would add that to the list of excuses she had heard over the years for obesity.

29th July

The doctor advised me that I had type 2 diabetes. She gave me literature to read and told me the dangers of diabetes if I did not take it seriously; lose weight, eat more healthily and exercise. Told to book in to see the diabetes nurse who would be 'looking after me'.

31st July

There is a fish supper and quiz night at the village hall. The idea is to raise funds for something or other. It never became obvious which local charity or good cause was to be the beneficiary. It didn't really matter. It was a night out and the chance to socialise. A good night was had by all. We did quite well in the quiz. There were about 18–20 tables of six people, and we were one of the few tables left at the end going head-to-head to be the winner. Unfortunately, my answer to the question, 'Where do women have the fuzziest hair?' was wrong. Apparently, the answer was Fiji. My wife and the people on my table were not amused by my answer. One or two chaps on other tables obviously agreed with me by their encouragement and clapping.

2nd August

Over the past few days, we have had tremendous winds and rain. Many areas of the country have had floods and structural damage with several roads closed due to being under water or over hanging trees in danger of falling. We have had fence panels uprooted. I drove to the local shops for top up supplies. I cannot believe my eyes! At the top of the road where I live was a council worker. Had to be council, hard hat, goggles, ear muffs, yellow fluorescent jacket. What is that in his hand? Oh yes, it is a leaf blower. This member of the human race was using his petrol driven leaf blower to blow leaves from the pavement and driveway leading to the crematorium. This chap was trying to blow leaves away in the face of 60 mph plus winds. The leaves were being blown back over his head and exactly to where they had come from. This was so stupid; I wanted to stop the car, get out and look for the TV cameras; surely, this was a spoof being filmed? As I was at a road junction, I could not stop, but how ridiculous. I would like to believe a high-ranking executive with braid and a peak cap scheduled this area to be cleared of leaves some two months ago and had no perception of prevailing weather conditions. No one surely this morning could have ordered this fellow onto the streets to perform a task of such monumental stupidity even King Canute would have laughed.

5th August

Pouring with rain, but there is food shopping to be done. We drove to the local Tesco superstore. I found a space in the disabled parking area but an adjacent car was badly parked, and there was little room for me to reverse into the available space and allow Hazel to open the door and get out. The plan was to let her out of the car and then for me to reverse into the space, unload and assemble her mobile scooter. Hazel got out of the front passenger side door and closed it. Looking carefully over my shoulder and in my rear-view mirror, I reversed. Whoops, scream, thud. Hazel had disappeared from view. I stopped the car, got out, went around the other side of the car and found Hazel lying on the ground. It was still pouring with rain, and she was sitting in a puddle. The Tesco staff were brilliant. Blankets were produced to keep her warm and as she had a pain in her head and been 'knocked over' by a car, it was decided to leave her on the ground and not move her. The ambulance arrived very quickly, and Hazel's injuries were inspected and treated. The ambulance men lifted her into the ambulance for further observation and treatment. I am left wondering how anyone could get out of a car, close the door and still be close enough to the car to be caught by the wing mirror and dragged to the ground? Guess what happens when a pedestrian is hit by a car? Oh yes, the police are called. A police squad car arrived and investigations get underway. The police questioned my wife, the ambulance men and try to see if any of the bystanders or Tesco staff can add evidence to this dastardly crime scene. "We would like you to undergo a breath test." It is still raining 'and for my convenience' the police would like us to go into the store where it is dry. Yes. There are crowds of people coming in and out of the store and just sheltering out of the rain. So, in truth, I am taken to most visible place on the entire retail complex to blow into the Breathalyzer. How many eyes are looking at me? It is 10.30 in the morning and I am being breathalysed. Of course, it shows a zero reading, and I am informed the police 'will not be taking any further action against me'. Hold on, how about charging my wife for diving underneath the car and giving me all this grief?

We proceed and do our shopping amid a continual debate as to who has ruined whose life, who was at fault. Hazel's final comment was I hit her with a lethal weapon. I remind her that it is impossible for anyone to close a car door and remain with three inches of the car so to be dragged back by the wing mirror.

9th August

We have some gift vouchers that had been given to us. We drove into Worthing as they have a wide selection of 'brand name' stores. While Hazel was looking around the Ladies department of a well-known store, I went to the Food Hall and picked up some bananas. I went towards the checkouts to see long queues on most aisles, but one checkout had a sign above it, 'Baskets only'. I went up to the lad at the till and said, "I don't have a basket; I only have some bananas." He looked at me as if I were mad, shook his head and asked if I wanted a bag.

I caught up with Hazel in the Lingerie Department. I followed behind her mobile trolley as she weaved in and out of the aisles. I must admit never to be quite at ease in the ladies' underwear section. I often catch the eye of ladies fondling thongs and bras and feel if I spoke or smiled it would be totally inappropriate, so, head down and study the wheels of Hazel's trolley. "Can I help you with something, sir?" said a voice from my side. I looked around and saw a young and extremely attractive lady shop assistant. The menu of things she could do for me ran through my mind. "Yes, I'd like a bacon sandwich, please," I said. Apparently, this was not a service she could provide so made her excuses and left me to follow Hazel's trolley.

12th August

This morning, we were scheduled to collect three picture frames we had specially made for three prints we had of Hong Kong. We lived there for four years in the middle to late '70s and the prints reminded us of happy times and how different the island was now, following a huge number of new skyscrapers being built. We have had a lot of rain in the area but were rather disappointed but not surprised when we came across a police road block and road closed signs about 400 yards from our destination, a hotel just outside of Chichester. I drove around the roundabout, turned off and thought I would try and go, right, right, right and come in from behind the hotel to where we were heading, obviously sticking to fairly main roads. We got to where I judged that one more right turn would lead us onto the correct road. Yellow florescent jackets everywhere! Road closed. Herbert in peak cap walked up to the car and asked us to turn around. I noticed from my milometer I had covered just short of four miles and now was being asked to turn back. Big flood I thought I had not realised just how close to us the flooding had come. "This road will be closed for about another half an hour," said Jobsworth. It didn't strike me immediately the precision of his statement, and I prepared to reverse and go home as there seemed no way to get to the hotel. "The runners should be through here by then," offered Jobsworth, as if to placate me. It was then that my self-control deserted me.

"So, these road closures from Westhampnett through Chichester to Summerdale have not been due to flooding but to bloody runners on the road, I pay road tax to use?" Hazel was good; she did try to calm me down, but I could see she was closer to seeing the humorous side to events than I was.

"The road should be clear now if you head back into Chichester," said Jobsworth. "They would have passed through there by now."

Four miles back to where we started from the roads were clear.

15th August

Today I saw the diabetes nurse and had a long chat about the sins of my past. We discussed an action plan of how I needed to accept that I had diabetes and it could kill me. I decided I really should work at eating salads, vegetables and fruit; cut out sweet things and do more exercise. She also gave me contact details for a specialist, day-long seminar on diabetes run by the Local Health Trust.

17th August

Went shopping today with Hazel, she wanted to buy a new dress. The first one in which she took an interest was a sort of terracotta at the hemline going up into a floral pattern. "You'll look like a plant pot in that," I said. The next dress was full of swirls and curls and was cut in such a way that I said, "You look like a sack of spuds in that." I thought I was being helpful and constructive, but all I got was:

"If you can't say anything nice just shut up!" We continued in silence. The air was still frosty when we moved into the Lingerie Department. Almost immediately, I saw a rather stunning lady in her late 20s, early 30s handling a thong. "You'll look great in that," I said. Apparently, that was wrong too.

20th August

Sticking to my new food regime and walking for about an hour a day. Losing weight. My trousers are getting very loose, belts have been tightened but I will need to buy some smaller trousers.

23rd August

Bought three pairs of trousers, no need for a belt.

26th August

We live about a mile from the sea and my daily walk consists of walking the same stretch of promenade day in day out. The weather changes, the tides change; it is a nice walk, but after a while, it gets a bit tedious.

1st September

One of the ladies with whom I play indoor bowls suggested I drove a few miles up the road and took the walk around a wetland harbour and wild life sanctuary. Speaking to Hazel back home, she said one of her friends at her knitting club also recommends the same walk. I am not much of a nature fan, bird watcher as such, but I thought I would give it a try for a change of scenery.

2ⁿᵈ September

Drove as instructed to find the new walk. I drove up an unmade-up road for about ten minutes. I don't know how far it was as I was going so slowly. I have never seen such deep and so many potholes. I drive a normal saloon car and was bouncing all over the place. I am sure lower slung sports cars would get grounded. This place is a nightmare. I eventually got to the end of this 'road'/'track' to find a gate across the road. CLOSED. Turned around and another ten minutes of bumping and scraping I arrive back where I started. Happy day.

10ᵗʰ September

Very high winds overnight have blown out a fence panel between my garden and my neighbour. Together, we popped it back into the grooved cement posts and all seemed well although we did notice a top strut of wood had broken. *C'est la vie.*

13ᵗʰ September

The high winds have continued and the fence panel has popped out again. My neighbour and I decide that the wooden strut across the top was obviously there for the purpose of keeping the fence panel rigid and now being broken the high winds allowed the panel to flex and pop out. It is my boundary fence, and I agree to buy a new one.

15th September

I went to B&Q to buy a fence panel. Due to the high winds, there had been a lot of local damage and they had run out. When I got home, it struck me I was never going to get the fence panel in my car and so in any event I would need to ask B&Q to deliver. Drove back to B&Q, ordered the fence panel to be delivered as and when. The salesman entered my order on his computer and produced an invoice. Not only did he produce an invoice but a nine-page document of Terms and Conditions! Nine pages. Whenever I have been into B&Q and bought whatever, I have paid at the checkout and been given a receipt. Seems a good system. But I now have an invoice and an additional nine pages of disclaimer. The girl at the checkout was as bemused as I. She said B&Q did so much for the environment she was amazed at this stupidity. I said that if I had three more pages I could probably have papered over the entire hole in the fence.

20th September

Very misty today. The weather forecast said something about dust from the Sahara blowing across Europe and the humid conditions hitting cooler air is causing pollution. I went for my daily walk along the sea front. Very eerie. Normally, you can see for miles, but today, the visibility was about 100 yards. There was a chap fishing off the beach. He had several rods out and all the equipment. Bloody fool, I thought to myself, how does he think the fish are going to see the bait under water and in this fog?

23rd September

Hazel was very ill this morning and asked me to call 999. The paramedics arrived within five minutes, brilliant. Hazel had trouble breathing, and they decided to take her to hospital. It was now about 8.30 am, and I was still not dressed. The ambulance went off blue light blazing, and I followed about fifteen minutes later and caught up with Hazel lying on a gurney in the A&E corridor with five other people. The A&E was full hence the back up. By 10.30, they opened up a side trauma ward and wheeled Hazel in putting her to bed. By 12.00, she still had not been seen by a doctor although her vital signs were being monitored. She asked for a commode. None arrived and eventually she wet herself. Reported the accident to a nurse. Sometime later, Hazel was wheeled into A&E, and by three o'clock, she was seen by a doctor. She was listed for x-rays and other tests. Hazel asked if she could have a drink as she had been brought into hospital just after 8.30 this morning and had not eaten or had anything to drink and by the way have been sitting in my own urine for the past three hours. X-rays and tests done, still no cup of tea. I saw a lady walking around the A&E asking people if they wanted a drink of tea or coffee. I managed to arrange for some tea for Hazel and myself. Hazel is now sitting in a chair in the curtained off cubicle as she can't stand lying in urine any longer. After complaining again about the bed to a nurse we had seen several hours earlier, she said she had asked someone to change the bed and was sorry no one had done it. She did it herself. Hazel got back into bed. She still had not been offered anything to eat all day. I went to the coffee shop and bought some sandwiches. Hazel had a headache, and I asked a doctor sitting at the reception desk for some Paracetamol. He said she would ask someone to find some. After about another two hours, Hazel was discharged and allowed home. Still, we never got the Paracetamol.

29ᵗʰ September

The phone went early this morning; it was our local doctor's surgery. The lady asked if I was still a full time carer for my wife. I confirmed that I was. She said they would like to offer me a free flu jab…

"Can I take the cash alternative please?" I said.

There was silence from the phone…

"Hello," I said. The lady was obviously confused by my request.

"Er, no we are offering you a flu jab for free as you are a full time carer."

"Excellent," I said, "but I would rather have the money."

"No, there is no cash alternative; it's a jab against the flu, that's all." I thanked her for her call, wished her a nice day and said goodbye…

2ⁿᵈ October

Went shopping this afternoon and among my list was a sink plug. I went to B&Q, a specialist plumbing store, our local hardware shop all were quite happy to sell me a 'kit' with plug, chain and all sorts of strange-looking stuff. Apparently, they all only sell the complete drainage package; no one sells a plug. Eventually, I went into Robert Dyas. I wandered about for a few minutes and couldn't see a plug. Resigned to hitting another blank, I asked the lady at the counter if they sold individual sink plugs. "Oh, yes, follow me." That's a result I thought, and I followed her down and around aisles to a wall full of gizmos and bits and pieces. "There you are, sir."

"Can you tell me please, which is for hot water and which is for cold?" I asked.

"I think they do both," she said with a very confused, not too sure, look on her face. I bought one, took it home, and it doesn't fit!

8th October

Decided to go out for dinner this evening and went to a French restaurant. One of those pretentious places where the menu is all in French. We seldom have duck at home as Hazel finds it too fatty. I fancied duck as a change so I asked the waiter what was the French for duck so I could find it on the menu. "Canard, sir," he said.

"Okay, if you don't know, go and ask someone else," I replied.

"No, sir, it is Canard."

"Look, chum, please don't use that language in front of my wife and go and ask the manager." I finished up having ouef and pommes frit.

15th October

I went to the Lamb at lunchtime and booked a table for dinner tomorrow night.

"May I book a table for dinner please for tomorrow?"

"Certainly, one moment I'll get the book."

"What is the largest party you can conveniently accommodate?"

"Almost any number, sir, we can move tables together as long as we know how many are coming. How many would be in your party, sir?"

"Two please, just me and the wife. Would you like some details?"

The young lady looked at me as if I were mad. "Yes, please."

"44-inch chest and 29-inch inside leg," I said.

Give the girl her due…"And what shoe size do you have, sir?"

I do like a little bit of repartee. Good on her.

17th October

Had a nice meal last night at the Lamb.

Hazel's mobility scooter is broken. I took it to the shop for repair. Hazel can't really go out without the scooter.

19th October

Retrieved the scooter, all mended.

23rd October

I received in the mail a renewal notice for my home emergency insurance cover. Not bricks and mortar, not contents but emergency burst waterpipes, breakdowns, etc. My premium had got from £108 to £168, and I had never made a claim. This sounded a rip off to me so I went online to compare prices. That was a joke. I can find house cover and contents cover but not emergency services cover. I eventually decide to telephone a company as I was fed up filling in registration details online only to find they could not offer what I wanted. I found cover for £130 and bought it over the phone. I now need to phone my current provider to say I wanted to cancel at maturity and not to automatically extend the cover. I spoke to a chap who was very polite and was English. I told him I wanted to close my insurance cover upon expiry. He of course asked why and I told him I thought an increase in premium of over 50% was scandalous. He asked would I stay if he held the premium at £108, which would in fact have saved me £22. I said 'No' as I felt if they could now offer to renew my policy at £108, they should have offered me that in the first place, not try and rip me off. He then, very professionally and politely said he could in fact reduce my premium to something around £28. I missed the exact figure as my mind could not comprehend that he had offered me a premium of £20 odd pounds instead of £168 they had demanded to roll over my policy. I could not believe what I was hearing and that there was no price at which I would renew the policy with his company if this was the business ethics and standards to which they worked. We politely parted in peace, and I actually complimented him in a customer service satisfaction survey at the end of the call. The guy was great; he is doing the job as he was trained, but I will never use that company again.

This now leads me to cancel my direct debit with my bank. To do things online, they always ask for my 'Transaction Code'. I do not have a 'Transaction Code' as this is based on my mobile phone number, and I do not have a mobile phone. Why is it these days everything you try to do revolves around a mobile phone? People want to text me messages and confirm things…No, I don't want people to text me, message me or whatever. I just want to get on with my life in a simple and uncomplicated manner. So, I need to phone my bank to cancel a direct debit. A robotic voice asks me to press 1 for this, 2 for that, 3 to wait a fortnight to speak to an imbecile…I am now asked for my telephone ID. I don't know what my telephone ID is, or even if I have one. When I don't answer the stupid cow in five seconds, she asks me again for my telephone ID. For some reason, my cool, gentlemanly politeness left me. "I don't have a f****** telephone ID," I shouted down the phone. After Mrs Robot asked another time for my telephone ID, I was told, she 'could not understand my answer' and I had to hold for the next available customer service operator. Eventually, I spoke to a human being and go through security checks. No problem, I understand they need to do security checks, but why make it so hard to get anything done. The person at the other end confirmed they had now stopped further payment of the direct debit and it would take 24 hours to take effect. Again, not a problem. I pay the premium monthly and checked when was the last payment; it was 15th October. My insurance runs out in December so I do need to pay the next and final premium to remain covered until the policy expires. I asked if I could cancel my direct debit after they paid next month's premium. 'NO', if I give them instructions to cancel, they will cancel it tomorrow and not pay further premiums. I said I needed them to pay the one due 15th November and cancel from then. Can't do it, I'll have to call back after the next payment is made, and they will cancel within 24 hours. The system does not accept future time frame cancellations! This is a F****** computer. You can tell a computer to do what you bloody well want it to do! Apparently, not.

1st November

Umpteen years ago at school, I knew a chap called Alan Brain. Nice enough chap but we never kept in touch after we left secondary school. I saw a large lorry today and thought of him. It had on the side 'Brain Removals'. Not the best marketing slogan I thought.

7th November

Hazel and I enjoy going out to lunch, and today, we went to a pub we had not been to before in Donnington. It had a good write up in the local paper. A lot of money had been spent on refurbishment, but to me, it lacked 'charm'. We ordered; Hazel asked for a burger, chips and the trimmings. She is slimming, you understand! I asked for chicken and mushroom pie. After what we considered rather too long, we were served. Hazel's meal looked fine. Mine came in an iron ramekin about one and half inches high by three inches wide. That was it. No veg, no side salad. That was it. I dug in with my knife and fork: No pie crust. The entire dish, or should I say pot, consisted of mash potato topping with a few pieces of chicken, a sliver of mushroom underneath. Hazel told me they could describe it as a pie as it has a potato mash topping over meat. I finished in no time at all. It tasted very nice but at just under £11. I thought it was an absolute rip off. I didn't even get a spoon to scrape the gravy from the bottom of the ramekin. I just had a knife and fork. Certainly, we shall not be returning, and I shall tell my local friends to avoid the Blacksmiths Arms at Donnington.

12th November

Travelling behind a tour bus on the way to Chichester; I am perplexed by the website address scripted on the rear. 'mytesticles.com'. Hazel corrected me. Apparently, it says, 'mystical tours.com'. Got to go to Specsavers.

17th November

We met our great friends Martin and Felicity for lunch at a nice pub on Hayling Island. Mart and Fea had always had dogs. Their most recent addition which they have had for over a year was another rescue dog from Spain, I believe. The dog was a nutcase! I am sure he thought he was a mixture of a chimpanzee and a hippopotamus. He would pull, jump, bark at anything and everything. What a change...He is now normal. Well done, you two, you have turned him into a loving pet. A proper dog. Not an animal!

25th November

I have found it hard to sleep recently. I have had a cold, can't breathe. You know what I mean. I went to the chemist and got some Nytol (other brands may be available). I read the paperwork inside the box. These are sleeping pills remember...'May cause drowsiness, tiredness...' 'Do not use when driving...' What kind of people write this stuff?

28th November

Not much luck with Nytol so I decided to get some Otravine. It's a sniff up the nose job. I went to the Tesco pharmacy counter and asked for some Otravine for my left nostril. She said all Otravine was the same and could be used up both nostrils. I said I had only one nostril blocked so could I have a smaller bottle just for the left side? No. It only comes in one size that does both sides. Can I have it for half price? I asked as I will only use one side. Apparently, not. I had to pay for the full, two nostril size.

30th November

I thought as I am out and alone, I'd start buying presents for Christmas for Hazel. Went to Poundland!

Hello again! It is now some 16 months since my dear wife Hazel suddenly passed away and my life hit a wall. I could not write; I could not draw my thoughts together and commit them to paper. Now, as life goes on, I have met Gill. We are together, and again my life has direction and meaning. We have sold our respective properties and have bought a house together. My tickle muscles and giggle bones have started to work again, so I thought I would take up my catalogue of life's traumas and trivialities. The following 'Catch up' section is a resume of the past months. Not in date order, but as I recollect them.

CATCH UP

The first time I stayed over at Gill's flat; in the morning, I went to the bathroom to do my bits and pieces, including brushing my teeth. I picked up a white tube with a red stripe on it, Colgate I thought. Squeeze, brush. No, it is not Colgate; it turned out to be a tube of Caniston thrush treatment!

I mentioned Gill sold her flat. The lady that bought it is a French national with a home in France. Her husband is quite seriously ill in hospital in England. She needed a British address to ensure her husband received continued NHS treatment and medical cover in England. I love the French!

Gill and I are currently renting a house in Elmer, West Sussex. We are buying a house together, but it will not be ready to occupy until about July as it is tenanted. The house we are in backs directly onto the beach. A lovely location, but it has no privacy. One of Gill's great hobbies is washing! She is not a great fan of tumble dryers. Having lived in a flat for several years and now, having a garden, she has a fascination for that age old phenomenon, the washing line. As I said, the house backs directly onto the beach. It is very often busy with dog walkers, joggers and people just out strolling along the beach. A couple of weeks after we moved in, we began to notice a regular crowd of men gathering whenever Gill strung out her knickers and bras. A free membership to the Elmer Working Men's Club was put through the door in recognition. The sailing club were not as appreciative. They sent rather a firm note asking Gill not to hoist her bras up on the line as the brightly coloured undergarments were distracting the sailors who, thinking they were signal flags, often crashed onto the rocks.

Following the death of a spouse, there is a lot of paperwork. The TV licence being one case in point. I needed to cancel the existing direct debit, which happened to be in Hazel's name. I e-mailed the required site to affect the cancellation and was told, I could not cancel it as it was not in my name. Only the licence holder had the authority to cancel a direct debit for the licence! My return e-mail pointed out that the licence holder, my wife Hazel, had passed away and I was moving house, hence the request to cancel the licence. Their response was the same, "Sorry, only the account holder can cancel."

My reply has been deleted from my files over the past few months, but in effect, I responded by saying: "In accordance with their request that my wife gives the order to cancel the TV licence direct debit, I shall visit the site where her cremated ashes were scattered and sweep up as much as I can. I shall pile all the sweepings together and wave a magic wand. If by some miracle my wife appears from the pile of ashes, twigs, gravel and leaves, I shall ask her to contact you directly." A few days later, the TV Licencing Authority contacted me obligingly saying that in the circumstances they had cancelled by wife's direct debit.

5th April

I went to the newsagent this morning for my daily newspaper. I went in, got the paper and went to the counter. There were no other customers in the shop and no one behind the counter. I waited, I waited and waited. Eventually, a lady arrived full of apologies. "I didn't hear the doorbell," she said. "So sorry to keep you waiting."

"Not to worry," I said. "I did not come through the door; I came through the keyhole, which didn't trigger the bell."

"Who do you think you are, Bloody Aladdin?" she said, brilliant, love it. I'll be back. That's my kind of service.

8th April

Had some good news that the house we are buying will be available in early May. The tenants have found somewhere else to live and are happy to vacate early.

11th April

Dug out the surveyor's report on the house. He reported there are a few issues that should be remedied. I telephoned three general builders and two specialist flat roofers. Of the five calls (and these are business phone lines remember), I had four answer phone messages.

14th April

Seventy-two hours later and no replies to my four answer phone messages left of builders' lines, I made further calls and registered to an 'online' help service for builders. By the end of the day, I now have four people coming to give me estimates for various works after we have taken possession of the keys and the tenants vacated.

17th April

Run out of shaving foam. I took out a new can Gill had bought. Different brand, no glasses on…pressed the squirt nozzle to be covered in foam, face, chest, tummy, floor and hand. I was holding the can the wrong way around.

30th April

Collected the keys from the vacating tenants and look around the house. Disappointed how dirty it looks. The garden and front drive are very, very weedy and overgrown. The whole house is dirty. One toilet in particular! Yuck.

2ⁿᵈ May

First batch of builders come to look at the work required and give quotes. We start weeding the garden and paths.

7ᵗʰ May

We have arranged for a professional firm of cleaners to come in and clean the house. We will deduct any costs from the tenants' deposit.

16ᵗʰ May

Moving day…no trauma…YET.

Late afternoon and the movers have just left. My attention is drawn to a man coming towards me from across the road. Hand outstretched. "My name is Julian and welcome to the street. It is my new neighbour from across the road." Nice chap. He proceeded to tell me all about the other neighbours, the neighbourhood and the history of our new house.

"Did you know about 15 years ago your house was a brothel?" Not an awful lot you can say to that. He proceeded to tell me the owner before last was a bit of a rogue. It seems in the early 2000s, the police had stationed themselves in Julian's two upstairs bedrooms for over three months, observing the comings and goings at our new home. It seems Mr Rogue was into drugs, dodgy cars and prostitution.

I eventually returned indoors to tell Gill. We then viewed the house in a different light. The stage in one bedroom could have given us a hint of irregular proceedings. The stage, perhaps 14 ft by 8 ft and some 6 inches high made of good wooden planks, stained walnut brown. Never previously had given it a thought. We moved into another room. There were 36 raw plug holes in the ceiling and floor. When originally viewing the house, we never noticed these holes in the ceiling and certainly not the floor as furniture would have covered most of them. Oh, that mirror is rather large for a room this size! In the garden, there are seven brick pillars built in a circle some 20 ft in diameter. Thinking laterally, a perfect base for a wooden dais or dance floor. There is a wrought iron spiral staircase that connects the garden to the upstairs balcony and three upstairs rooms. Looking now more closely as we moved around our new and lovely new home, Gill noticed that most doors not only had keyhole locks but bolts as well on the doors.

Why on earth did our vendor live here for 15 or so years leaving all these trappings in situ?

I think that is enough excitement for one day and so to bed perchance to dream!

19ᵗʰ May

Just about finished opening the boxes and taking cardboard, bubble wrap and newspaper to the dump. Now to continue in the garden. We have four pairs of secateurs between us, and they are in for some heavy-duty work. They are not much good, so I decided to go to Wicks and buy a new pair. At the checkout, I am holding two sets of secateurs. "Which one is left-handed and which one right-handed?" I asked the checkout girl giving her the two pairs. She looked stunned.

"Oh, I don't know; I'd use them like this," she said holding one pair and demonstrating deft hand movement.

"Okay, I'll take both pairs then, please," I said.

23ʳᵈ May

I went into Rustington today and bought some 'stuff' from a factory outlet type of shop. "Are you a club member?" asked the checkout girl.

"Oh, you are a club are you? Do you have a bar and restaurant? Do you organise day trips?" I asked. The young lady looked rather shocked.

"No, it's just that you get points if you are a member."

24ᵗʰ May

Every two weeks, Gill and I go to a Meet Up group where we have a chicken supper and then play ten pin bowling. Usually, there are about 12–14 of us. Probably 8–10 being a core of regulars and then there are those who come every now and again. On this occasion, I was sitting opposite a lady I had not seen before. I think it was her first visit to the group. We were talking socially around the table and most of the regulars there knew Gill and I had just moved, and we were asked how we were getting on in our new home. We said that our house backed onto Mewsbrook Park in Littlehampton. The house was lovely; there was a lot of work we wanted to do, but we were very pleased with it and looking forward to years to come. We were having the balcony repaired and spiral staircase removed as our first major project. "Yes, it used to be a brothel," said the lady opposite me. Rather a conversation stopper at the dinner table. This lady lived 20–30 miles away from Littlehampton, but from my description of the house, she knew exactly where it was and confirmed it was a well-known house 15–20 years ago. Apparently, friends of hers had looked over the house some several months earlier with the intention of buying it.

27th May

Lovely day today, sitting in the garden taking it easy but can smell a malodorous pong! It smells very much like a sewer. First thoughts are the drains are blocked. On the phone and call out a drains man to CCTV the drains and do what is necessary.

29th May

Electrician came today and fitted two new fuse boxes and sorted out other bits. We have a fish pond that we have decided is not something we wish to retain. We have sliced up the liner and allowed the water to drain out. Garden cuttings and other rubbish is being put into the pond with the idea of getting more hardcore in, then fill it with soil and make an alpine garden or rockery.

2nd June

Man with hardcore and soil arrives, dumps everything into the 'pond'. We went to a garden centre and bought several alpine bits and pieces. The words 'Manager's Special' and 'Sale' seem to hold a fascination for Gill.

4th June

Our neighbour Tim came around this morning. "I have a man from the Environment Department at the Council coming this afternoon about the smell coming from the stream in the park. Would you like to come over and see him and see what can be done about the smell?"

I've just spent the best part of £800 on getting the drains swept and the smell apparently is from a stream at the bottom of his garden, but as we are next door, the smell wafts across. Brilliant.

9th June

The roofer starts today. They are to clean the roof of moss, re-point the ridge tiles and clean out the valleys. They are to re-roof the garage, which leaks badly and reconfigure the balcony at the rear of the house.

12th June

Work on the roof seems to be going well, but they left early today as it was 'too hot' to work on the balcony!

At this time, let me explain about the balcony. I have previously said the balcony runs the width of the house at first floor level. It crosses the upstairs kitchen, a lounge and a bedroom. It is some 45 ft long by maybe 8 ft wide and is accessed by three sliding patio doors from the three rooms and also from the wrought iron spiral staircase from the garden. The floor surface is made of the tarmac/felty stuff that when it gets hot you can dig holes in it! Given the colourful history of the house, you can image the amount of stiletto heels, table and chairs' legs being dug into it over the past 40 odd years.

It looks dreadful, but it works. It also slopes inwards and drains via an internal downpipe, which downstairs is hidden in a wall. Sounds strange but you cannot see the downpipe and the water drains away efficiently.

In getting estimates to redo the balcony, all the roofers invited to quote suggested reconfiguring the balcony to slope away from the house and fit a guttering system around the house to catch the rainwater as it flows off the balcony. This sounds a good idea, very logical and every quote was to do just that. Reconfigure the balcony to slope away from the house and fit a new gutter to catch the water.

14th June

We are getting the first feelings that not everything is going to plan with the balcony. A skip is ordered and a huge amount of debris is taken away. I am advised the balcony has been constructed over two or three different times as the joists, rafters and whatever else is under the roof are of different heights and thicknesses. What do I know? I am a layman paying the bill for a specialist to do his job. Get on with it!

15th June

It rained last night and water came through the ceiling of the downstairs lounge. We put out a couple of pots and pans to catch the drips. Obviously, when the workmen covered up last night, they did not do a very good job. We phoned the bloke; he offered to come out, but what's the point? We were catching the drips, upset, disappointed; but what can you do? This morning, I expected the boss man to knock on the door and apologise for what happened, ask to see where it happened, grovel perhaps, at least show some modicum of interest in what happened. I live in a dream world obviously. Not a word from the boss man.

19th June

I am told the balcony is finished. Workmen run off. They obviously have spent more time and money on the balcony than was envisaged. They do not 'test' the balcony and guttering; they just scoot off, obviously to another job.

21st June

It rained last night…The balcony is awash with standing water. We venture onto the balcony and sweep off the puddles into the guttering.

Oh, no, we don't! We sweep the water off the balcony and down the side of the house as the gutter is too far away from the edge of the balcony to catch the water.

Phone call made. I have not paid my specialist flat roofer for his work.

22nd June

Roofer returns and slaps more fibreglass on the balcony along the house wall hoping the increased height will give sufficient camber to allow the water to run off. They also have another go at the gutters.

24th June

We have a little more rain, and it is obvious the balcony is still too flat to allow water to run off. I phoned the chartered surveyor who gave me the initial report on the house before we purchased it. I wanted to ask his advice as to my legal position and what were his thoughts as to how to proceed.

27th June

Surveyor turned up unannounced. Never mind. He obviously can see the balcony is too flat. He said the only way to get the camber required was to raise the height from the ground of the three patio doors. At this time, the three doors are almost flush with the balcony floor. I can see the logistical problem. It now occurs to us we will need to replace three double-glazed sliding patio doors, which we had not bargained for. Money, money, money.

28th June

We were awakened last night at 1.45 in the morning with a thump. The noise came from upstairs. I went up thinking maybe a picture had fallen off a wall. No, I could see nothing that could have caused the noise. Downstairs, back to bed. Thump. Half past three. Both Gill and I now went upstairs. We could see nothing out of the ordinary. I opened a patio door and went out onto the balcony. Crack, crunch…The floor was cracking under foot. We could do nothing but go back to bed and wait for the morning to call our favourite roofer man.

29th June

Mr Roofer boss man came. He can see he has not done the job required, nor indeed for which he has estimated. He said the cracking of the balcony floor was the resin covering cracking. The underlying fibreglass was watertight and the house would not get wet. The fact the guttering did not work was because the facia boards of the house were not true. The balcony was not as required due to the lack of height with which he had to work when laying the balcony floor due to the patio doors being so low. I pointed out to him that the chartered surveyor had commented that while he had the roof stripped in the first place, he should have seen he did not have the necessary camber to do the job as quoted. He could, at that time, have raised the point with me and with my agreement, run a ridge the length of the balcony allowing half the water to run back into the existing down pipe in the house. The other side of the ridge would be high enough to run off into the gutters. We are talking millimetres in the height required, not something that would be obtrusive.

Gill and I appreciate he has lost money on this job. He has spent far too long and spent additional money on materials. Business is business. In life, you take your knocks. I said to him this situation is not what either of us wanted. I offered him £300 cash to walk away, and I would get another firm to have another go at the roof. I said we were going to get three new doors fitted to allow extra height for the balcony to slope away. He would not take the £300 and said he 'would seek advice'.

2nd July

A salesman from Everest came to measure up and quote for three new patio doors. He started at £19,999 and finished at £10,000 and some. A second double-glazing man arrived, quoted, and we found his price to be acceptable. We are going ahead with them.

Having now committed to spending money for which we had not budgeted, we felt in need of refreshment. We went to Establo, a new wine bar / cafe just opened in Rustington. It used to be a petrol garage so it has a very large forecourt with several tables, chairs, umbrellas and heaters outside. Inside is large and shabby chic in decor. We sat just inside at a comfortable table people watching. Just the other side of the window was a table with three people, two youngsters, maybe twenty somethings and an elderly lady, possibly one of their grandmothers? The mature lady was certainly in her very late 70s, possibly 80s. Her face had more lines than a weather map. Her hair was a mixture of purple, grey and blue. She was heavily made up with lots of bling. She wore a white lace short bolero over her blue T-shirt, and she was obviously wearing a very short skirt judging by the amount of leg she was showing. After a while, the two youngsters left. The lady finished her drink, lit what was almost certainly a joint by the size of it. She finished that and came inside. As she stood up, you could see her short skirt was in fact a micro skirt. It was not a mini; this was outrageous. She was wearing three-inch stiletto heels. She came in clutching a cushion on which she had been sitting and replaced it on a chair close to us and tottered off to the Ladies'. When she came back, she wished us a nice evening, said goodbye and tottered across the forecourt and onto a mobility scooter and away…Gill and I roared with laughter, what a girl? She possibly lived half a mile away, didn't want to walk that far, didn't want the expense and hassle of driving a car while having 'a good time', so a mobility scooter it was. Why not? Brilliant. Good on you girl.

4th July

Mr Roofer wants to continue the job and will be present when the double-glazing surveyor is here to measure up. Awaiting for a date.

5th July

It poured with rain again last night. The rear garden outside the annex was flooded. I called the drains people.

6th July

Drains man says the soak away is full and we need a new one. Money, money, money.

9th July

More rain. The front drive is flooded. I phoned the drains man. They are coming in early September to dig out and fit a new soak away in the rear garden. He says we need another in the front garden. Money, money, money.

We have a new drive being laid in the front. My thought process goes…spend loads of money on the new drive then in September the drains people come in and dig up a portion of the front drive to build a soak away then, unskilled guys relay my drive and probably bugger up my guarantee!

The surveyor for the double-glazing company was due to measure up for the patio doors. He has phoned to say his wife has been taken into hospital and cannot come here today. We should get a call from his office to rearrange the visit.

10ᵗʰ July

I discuss this scenario with both the drains people and the driveways guys. They both suggest and I agree, that the drains people will do the back garden soak away in August and the drive people will fit a new soak away. That is a good deal.

12ᵗʰ July

Phone call from double-glazing surveyor; he will be here on Wednesday. Mr Roofer agrees to come too so he can discuss the door fittings and how he can liaise with the fitters and install a watertight seal between the door bases and the balcony. Apparently, a lead tray needs to be fitted between doorframe and the balcony to ensure a good seal.

14ᵗʰ July

Double-glazing surveyor arrived to measure for fitting the three new patio doors. Mr Roofer not here. I phone him…He thought it was next week! I look at my e-mail confirming to him the date. Sure enough, this Wednesday. How on earth Mr Roofer thought it was next week, I have no idea.

I e-mailed Mr Roofer to ask for clarification as to how he will fit the lead trays. Can he come here, measure up, buy and configure the lead tray so when the double-glazing people take out the doors he can fit the lead trays?

15ᵗʰ July

Mr Roofer replies to my e-mail saying the patio doors need to be removed; he then measures up, buys the materials then fits the lead trays. I smell a rat. My thoughts and indeed my e-mail reply to Mr Roofer were along the lines of: 'Surely, you cannot be serious? Are you saying that the double-glazing guys need to remove all three doors, then you measure all three doors as they are certainly different sizes. Then you will leave site go to the local builders' merchant and buy the lead and other materials needed. Meanwhile four double-glazing guys are sitting here drinking tea and twiddling their thumbs waiting for you. Sods law the builders' merchant you first visit will not have the right sort of lead, the right amount of lead, the right ****** colour lead whatever. I can see the probability of being here for three weeks with no doors on the upstairs three rooms. This cannot be happening!'

16ᵗʰ July

The guys putting down the new drive seem to be doing a good job. Small issue in that often the top man is called away to another site. They would do more work if they all stayed here and got on with the work.

Phone call from double-glazing company giving me a date they will fit the windows. E-mailed Mr Roofer to advise him date of fitting and pleading he will be here and asking for his comments on my e-mail.

18ᵗʰ July

Mr Roofer confirms he will be here on fitting date and that he will measure after the windows have been removed. He knows what he is doing, and it won't take him long to go to the local Travis Perkins and buy what is needed.

20th July

Today was a 'Footgolf' event held by Worthing Meetup group. It is played the same as golf but using footballs which you kick towards and into holes. Obviously, the holes are large enough to receive the footballs. Turn up late due to workmen being late arriving and late leaving. Thirty-six men and women are playing in six groups. Well organised, majority are aged in their 50s or 60s. Guess who won with the lowest score? Yes, me. Very pleased. Gill and I went for a coffee in the cafe. We were joined by Zoggy, yes, Zoggy who is a 60-something lady. We were chatting away, exchanging views on the event and people we each knew. Suddenly, she brought out a ham and lettuce sandwich and proceeded to eat it. We are sitting in the middle of the café, and she is eating a homemade sandwich!

22nd July

We are now into day 10 of laying the drive. The drive looks good, but it is not finished. There are slabs within the front porch that need to be laid and small areas of the wall need finishing. Not a lot, but the guys have been here for four days longer than estimated, and for the last three days, they have been here on and off for thirty minutes to a couple of hours a day before they leave for another job, or certain things they need are not here. It is now past 11.00 and no one is here and no phone call explaining why no one is here. I feel an e-mail coming on!

I have sent an e-mail expressing my disappointment at the lack of progress with the drive and pointing out that next week, we have scaffolders here, drains people, the doubleglazers and Mr Roofer. I told them that I did not have an inexhaustible supply of cups and could their people bring their own next week as I did not have enough to go around. Received an e-mail about 14.00 saying Martin will be here soon. Martin has arrived within moments; 16.00 and Martin says he has to leave to buy some pointing stuff to go between the floor slabs in the front porch. Yes, they do need pointing, but why on earth was he not supplied with the stuff before he came here? I am not upset; I am not upset...

25ᵗʰ July

Drive finished and looking good. Scaffolding erected for patio doors. What could go wrong?

26ᵗʰ July

Mr Roofer arrives bright and early, ahead of the patio door people. He parked deep into the drive so I said he should probably move his lorry out onto the street as he will be blocked in when the patio door people arrive. He will need to drive out having measured up for the lead trays then go and buy what is needed.

"Oh, that's okay. I have everything I need!"

I did not say a word, but my mind was racing, and I pinched myself to see if I was dreaming. This is the guy with whom I had been corresponding debating the fact he had to measure up for what he need after the windows were removed. This guy is seriously a nutcase, or he has been deliberately winding me up about needing to measure after the windows had been removed. I held my silence. This is the guy who I need to relay the balcony properly.

End of the day, the windows have been replaced. Look fine, work well, the guys have left and Mr Roofer and his mate continue working on the balcony for a couple more hours. Mr Roofer is finished. I pay him an additional £500 cash in hand as agreed for the extra materials he needed. He says all should now be well. Don't go out on the balcony tonight as the resin needs to set. If, in future, following any rainfall there is any residual water, it will be under the handrail balustrade.

27ᵗʰ July

New day, new morning, we can now get onto the balcony the resin having set. The newly laid balcony floor has indeed been cambered some three inches higher against the house, under the new patio doors; it certainly slopes away towards the edge. But then it stops. The new balcony floor is a series of wooden sheets covered in resin. The idiot has cut the sheets twelve inches short of the balcony edge therefore ending against the balustrade legs as he was too lazy to cut the wooden sheets around the legs so as to finish at the edge. We are furious.

28ᵗʰ July

It rained overnight and guess what? We have several reservoirs of water approximately six feet by one foot under the balustrade! An e-mail of complaint swiftly followed. Mr Roofer responded asking for his account to be settled in full. I responded telling him the job had not been finished to my satisfaction and indeed he had not completed lining part of the guttering. I said I would pay him £1,500, which together with the £500 cash I had given him and previous monies paid, I considered this to be payment in full for the quality of service he had provided. Full documentation of our exchange of e-mails and a portfolio of several photographs showing the various stages of his incompetency were to hand if he wished to take matter further.

29ᵗʰ July

Scaffolding still here. I check my paperwork for the double-glazing and see they say then scaffolding will be here for between 24–48 hours.

30ᵗʰ July

Phoned double-glazing company and reported their scaffolding is still here.

1ˢᵗ August

Received a phone call from double-glazing company. Was I satisfied with their service/product, etc.? Would I write a recommendation of their service on their website? All okay, yes, I am pleased and will write a reference. Oh, by the way, your scaffolding is still here.

3ʳᵈ August

Scaffolding still here. Phoned company, please collect.

5ᵗʰ August

Received a phone call from the double-glazing company to advise me that they had received so many enquiries for business from people living around my address resulting from their job at my home; they were pleased to offer me a 40% discount if I wanted any further double-glazing done in the next twelve months. (Bullshit, just another sales ploy). Oh, by the way, your scaffolding is still here.

7th August

Scaffolding still here and I rang again asking them to remove it. Okay, will be with you between Tuesday and Thursday next week.

12th August

Thursday has been and gone and no sign of the scaffolders. I decide to send them an invoice for safe keeping and storage. £100 per week.

19th August

Scaffolding still here. I send another invoice with £100 brought forward and another £100 for safekeeping and storage.

22nd August

I receive a phone call from scaffolding company saying they will collect the scaffolding on Monday. "Sorry you can't, I have sold it." A muffled noise from the other end of the phone followed by a request that if I could hold on a manager would speak to me. A couple of minutes later, a voice from higher up the food chain came on the phone. Apparently, I have no right to sell the scaffolding as it is not my property. I related to her the three pro-active calls I had made to her company, the two requests made during their calls to me. The one promised and failed collection date of three days! My two invoices for storage and safe keeping were ignored. It seemed to me they did not want the scaffolding kept safely for them, and I felt I had every reason to sell the scaffolding. I did not know exactly when next week collection would be made, but I assured her I had sold the scaffolding. "We will be there on Monday between 9 and 11 am."

25th August

Bright and early, a lorry arrived and scaffolding collected.

28th August

Our garden plays host to several forms of wildlife, magpies and squirrels amongst them. This morning, a squirrel was on the lawn digging, probably for nuts or seeds. A magpie was standing two or three feet away. It makes a jump at whatever the squirrel had dug up; the squirrel, not to give up his trophy lightly, takes a swipe at the magpie who jumped away. This went on for over five minutes; the magpie jumping in on the squirrel's lunch and the squirrel taking a swipe at the magpie. Fascinating.

30th August

Not heard any feedback from Mr Roofer so I conclude he has decided not to press for the unpaid balance of his account.

3ʳᵈ September

For the last couple of days, we have had a large dog poo deposited in front of the door. We decided to go to Pets at Home and buy some dog repellent spray. Having decided upon a certain product, Gill paid at the counter. The salesman asked if she had a loyalty card. "No," said Gill, "I don't have any pets; this is because a dog has been shitting on my front door step."

Got home and sprayed the 'stuff' along the width of the boundary drive and in front of the house. Stinks of lemon.

4ᵗʰ September

At 6.30 this morning, Gill is wondering if the shitting dog has paid us a visit. I am doubtful, hoping the spray has worked its wonders.

"If the dog comes onto the drive, the security lights will go on, won't they?" said Gill.

"No, the security lights have a height sensor at about five foot to activate when a human being comes into the drive. It will not be activated when foxes, cats or dogs walk around. You would not want the light coming on and off all night every time a bird or fox walks by."

Not convinced by this fact, Gill, dressed only in her pink dressing gown, went out the front door, crawled around on her hands and knees acting like a dog trying to see if the light would be activated! Quite what anyone would have thought if they should have passed by! Now convinced the lights would not be activated by a dog, she kept vigil for ages, bowl of water to hand, daring any dog to come onto the drive.

9th September

Several days have now gone and no more dog poo. The spray seems to have done its job.

Received a phone call from the double-glazing company apologising for the misunderstanding over the scaffolding and agreed to pay me £50 in 'compensation'. I accepted.

11th September

Gill has some frozen dumplings by Aunt Bessie she wants to use in tonight's dinner. I was downstairs looking at Millwall play Birmingham on the television, and Gill was cooking in the upstairs kitchen. She had obviously come close to finishing as she came down to tell me dinner was almost ready. There was about five minutes left of the game, and she stayed watching with me. Final whistle, Millwall won 2–0. Funny smell! We went upstairs where the smell of burning and smoke became more and more acrid. The microwave was pouring smoke. Upon investigation, it seems Gill had misread the cooking instructions for the dumplings as 12 minutes not 1 minute. Doors and windows were opened, dumplings tossed in the bin. What takes twelve minutes in a microwave? You could probably cook a whole pig for goodness' sake in that time.

12th September

Received a cheque for £50 from double-glazing company.

15th October

Not a lot has happened in the past few weeks. We have today received a regular card from a holiday company with whom we have previously holidayed. They are advertising a five-day, four-night deal at several of their hotels. We have nothing on the cards so decided to book a short holiday in Newquay. Bed breakfast, evening meal and entertainment there and back by coach £149 pp.

28th October

Just got back from Newquay. We had a good time. A little windy one day. We could not find a place that did Cornish cream teas!

1st November

Went to our regular chicken supper and ten pin bowling evening with a group of friends. I scored seven strikes and two spares and totalled 210 points. My previous personal best was 174 so I was very pleased. I did nothing different from all the other games I have played and am usually pleased if I break 100.

2nd November

Found a leak coming from the skylight in the annexe roof. I went onto the roof and half the window is missing. We phoned around and overcoming the initial difficulty of finding a company that work with windows on flat roofs, have arranged for a chap to visit and see if they can repair it.

4th November

The window can be 'fixed', but the better job would be to fit a new lantern window. This would be about five times the size of the original window plus they would put in sunken ceiling lights and re-plaster the whole ceiling. Money. Money, money but we go for it.

8ᵗʰ November

Gill received a letter today from our favourite travel company. They are offering deals at three of their hotels. Five days, four nights, bed breakfast, evening meal and entertainment. £79 pp for the Regent Hotel in Weymouth. Pick up and return by coach. We jump at the offer calculating we could hardly stay at home for that money.

9ᵗʰ November

Gill phoned to book the five-day break. She said we would rather self-drive than be collected by coach. We did not expect any discount from the original price but preferred the flexibility of having our own transport to use when we were in Weymouth. Having travelled with them before, they usually offer £10 pp off for self-drive rather than going by coach. "That will be £134 pp."

"Sorry, your offer is £79 pp by coach. We want to self-drive and are happy to pay the full £79."

"Sorry, self-drive is £134 pp." A short discussion between Gill and myself confirmed that we would go by coach and pay £79 pp. Job done. I feel a letter to the business manager of the company must be written!

10th November

Dear sir,

My partner Mrs Gillian Chalcraft recently received notice of your excellent Tinsel & Turkey breaks. We have booked and shall soon enjoy five days with you in Weymouth.

On a previous break, we travelled on a 'self-drive' basis rather than travel by coach. Having now done both, we find the additional flexibility afforded by having one's own car to hand was advantageous.

On booking this latest holiday, Gillian asked if we could 'self-drive' rather than go by coach. She was advised that the break would now cost £134 per person to 'self-drive'. We booked to go by coach!

I have been in business for close to 50 years. I have lived and worked in Europe, the Middle East and Asia. I have lectured at university to masters, graduates in international finance and feel I am reasonably well versed in business techniques. I am at loss to understand how you can offer such a generous deal of £79 to be taken by coach and yet it will cost £55 each extra to travel under our own steam. If you can refer me to any published research into this business technique, I would be very much obliged.

Yours faithfully.

18th November

Back from our trip to Weymouth. All went well but no reply to my letter.

2ⁿᵈ February

Have a look at the date! Christmas and the New Year have come and gone. In the past couple of months, no one or nothing has wound me up to pass comment. The only observation I would make is that a seagull has chosen, for the past few days, to alight on the balcony and peck at the patio doors. Strange. Seagulls are big birds. The size of a large chicken. This thing pecks at the window, and we wonder if the people living here before fed it? We have been here for seven months now, and this has only just started, so I doubt that was the case.

5ᵗʰ February

A letter has arrived from our coach travel company. They are offering a 'Buy one get one free' deal to several of their hotels. We chose to go to a hotel in Torquay for five days, four nights. It is £99 for the two of us! Not each, for the two of us. Bed, full breakfast, three-course evening meal with entertainment each night. We booked to go away from next Sunday. We did not ask about self-drive!

12ᵗʰ February

Back from Torquay. Terrific value, very hilly. We went to a pretty village outside Torquay called Cockington. I used to play a lot of cricket at a good level and have played at some really nice grounds. The Cockington village ground is in a bowl. The square in the middle seems reasonably flat but the outfield rose all around the effect being that the boundaries must have been 30–40 feet higher than the table. It must be interesting chasing down the ball in the outfield for its momentum then to run out and for the ball to stop and run down the hill again past the poor fielder running after it. I can image some fun times in the outfield!

3ʳᵈ March

The weather has improved a little, and we spent some time in the garden cutting down trees, cutting back some shrubs, weeding and digging around generally. Prior to being diagnosed with diabetes, I was a couple of stone heavier and wore trousers with 42-inch waist. I now use a pair as my gardening trousers. I am down to a 34-inch waist so they are very loose fitting, but with a belt, they hang in there and being quite thick are good for gardening. Having chopped down a fir tree, the trunk was cut to about a 15-foot length, which Gill and I were going to take to the dump with a load more rubbish. We needed to take the trunk through to the front drive and into my car. We each held one end of the truck and walked it across the lawn. After a few steps, I felt my trousers being to slip down, another two steps and down they went around my ankles. I couldn't walk holding the trunk with the trousers around my ankles so I called to Gill to stop and rest. She turned, saw my plight and roared with laughter. Not a bit of sympathy, pity or commiseration, just outright crying with laughter.

7ᵗʰ April

Doesn't time fly?

I have said I have diabetes type 2 and as such have a medical twice a year. My 'invitation' arrived this morning. I am due for a blood test on 24ᵗʰ April.

"Please bring an early morning, non-fasting urine sample in a white-topped bottle when you arrive."

Not unusual, standard procedure but I have always been asked to obtain a sterilised sample bottle from reception in which to provide the sample. I felt this deserved a personal visit to the surgery to discuss the options if a 'white topped' bottle was unavailable. After a short queue, it was my turn at reception where I produced my 'invitation' letter and pointed out the request for the sample to be delivered in a white-topped bottle.

"My milk bottle has a green cap; my mayonnaise has a blue lid and my wine bottles tend to be either black or gold caps. The only white-topped bottle I can think I use is a ketchup sauce bottle but that will not be empty before 24th April. Can you suggest what I can use?"

"You can use one of these, but there is a 20p deposit," the receptionist replied, giving me a proper sanitised sample bottle. I do appreciate a bit of repartee.

30th July

We have had a splendid summer so far and no one has upset me or wound me up for a while. Hence it is now the end of July. I was reading the newspaper this morning and chanced upon a headline that says you should have sex at 10.00 pm. Intrigued as to whether this should be on the bus, an underground train or maybe the local chippie, I read on. Apparently, it was an article setting out at which times of day your body is most receptive to certain things. Immediately, I am thinking this is c**p, but I'll read on. It gave a whole list of times from 6.00 am around the clock to 5.00 am the next day setting out your body's chemical reaction to time, food and rest, etc. Yes, it said that 10.00 pm was the optimum time for sex for a 50-year-old and 10.20 pm if you were 40! Who the hell writes this stuff and gets paid for it? There was no advice or suggestion as to the routine of a 70-year-old whose partner is 50. Perhaps the 50-year-old starts by themselves at 10.00 pm and the 70-year-old joins in at about 11.00 pm. What absolute drivel?

My hall roof is leaking, a down pipe in the garden is blocked and the central heating service man has not turned up. Apparently, my address was not on his call list today. A bloke is on his way from half an hour's drive away, and it is now three hours since the scheduled appointment. Maybe the world has caught up with me. It has been quiet too long.

3rd January

Recently had a letter requesting me to attend Littlehampton Hospital for my diabetes eye test. My turn arrived, and I was asked to 'take a seat'. I sat behind a desk upon which was an eye test machine. After initial questions and a normal 'close one eye and read from the card' test, I was asked to rest my chin on this fancy machine. There was an obvious grooved cup on which it was intended to 'rest my chin'. So far so good. "Look at the spot in the lens and open wide." I looked at the spot in the lens and opened wide. Problem was I opened my mouth wide. I was supposed to open my eyes wide. I suppose I have been to the dentist more times than an eye hospital, but it just was a natural reaction to open my mouth when asked 'Open wide'. Words were exchanged…

10ᵗʰ January

Gill has a small Mazda car bought new ten years ago. She received a letter today from Mazda asking her to make an appointment with her local Mazda dealership as there was a problem with the bolts securing the driver's seat. Gill phoned and got an appointment. The chap at the dealership obviously was well aware of this type of issue; I am sure he had already had several similar calls and Mazda themselves would have alerted all dealerships of the product recall. The chap told Gill he was well aware of the issue and had received several calls about seat bolts and air bags…Gill said she had not received a letter about air bags and went ahead and made an appointment to take the car in next Monday.

18ᵗʰ January

Three days after Gill had her seat bolts secured, she received a letter from Mazda advising of a product recall on her car for faulty airbags!

Why on earth can't the left hand speak to the right hand? Gill now has to arrange another dealership visit.

19ᵗʰ January

Earlier this month, I wrote to the NS&I. I have held premium bonds since I was a child and not won anything for certainly over 50 years. I thought it time to reconcile my holdings and sell up. I know my parents had several bonds too, so I asked the NS&I if the bonds they held were still valid. My father died in 1986, my mother in 2003. I honestly did not know if, upon their deaths their holdings were sold or if the whole issue was overlooked. I just wanted to check. I submitted three forms, one in each name and on my parents forms I wrote 'deceased' after their names. Obviously in my covering letter I also said they were dead.

Today, I received three letters, one telling me they could not divulge any information about my father's holdings and asking if he could write, asking for the information. One telling me they could not divulge anything about my mother's holdings and asking that she too write asking for this information. A third letter showing a list of the bonds I hold. I telephoned NS&I to discuss the situation and was told to send copy death certificates and more forms which are specific to notify NS&I of a holder's death. I spent a couple of hours finding and copying the death certificates and downloading and filling in the relevant forms from the NS&I website.

22ⁿᵈ January

Today, I received three letters from NS&I. One listing the entire portfolio of premium bonds which were held by my father and advising they are no longer valid. Another letter listing specifically the entire portfolio of my mother's holdings, no longer valid and a third letter saying they were sending separately yet another letter showing my holdings. I am quite satisfied that upon the deaths of my parents their holdings were liquidated; that is not an issue. But what an administrative cock up sending six letters when one would do, and I am apparently still expecting another. What is it about left and right hands?

23rd January

Two more letters from NS&I. One listing, as promised, my holdings of premium bonds exactly the same, word for word as their letter received last week. Guess what? The second letter informed me I had won £25 in the October and December 2018 draws. I thought this demanded a return letter. I wrote requesting they pay my winnings into my bank account and gave them the bank, sort code, account number, etc. I further expressed my incredulity into the fact that, for over 50 years I had won nothing, then as soon as I contact them I find I have won twice within the past three months! I requested they explore their unclaimed winnings file to see if I had previously won anything. I accept I have lived abroad for some years and since returning to England I have moved several times. I have not kept NS&I informed of these changes of address. I apologised and said I hoped they could do the required research on my behalf. The letter I had written earlier today with a form requesting the sale of and enclosing my actual bonds, has been retrieved from the sideboard and held pending further news…

7th February

Just returned from a few days away in Weymouth. Gill received an 'offer' from the holiday company we have used frequently, and they were offering five days half board in Weymouth for £59. We could hardly stay at home and go out each day for breakfast and three-course dinner for that money. Plus, evening entertainment and half-price drinks at the bar on the first and last night. It was again very good value. However…as we were about 400 yards from the hotel, I felt the car acting a little strangely, and yes, I had a puncture. I thought we were so close to the hotel, I would drive there, claim a car parking space and get a call out repair man. We did book in and secured car park place. I asked the parking attendant where was the local tyre shop. He pointed out Kwik Fit, and we walked around to see them. They said they could replace the tyre, but I'd have to bring the car into their garage. I asked if they did a mobile fitting service as I wasn't too happy to drive the car to their shop. They gave me a number who was Kwik Fits mobile service to be told they do not do emergency call outs on weekends, the best they could do was Tuesday. I decided to risk driving around from the hotel to the garage. I did this and two people kindly pointed out to me that I had a flat tyre! When my car was hoisted on the ramp, I was told the wheel locking nut was not for my Ford but was for a BMW. That could only have happened when the last time I changed a tyre at National Tyres they switched my key by mistake for another car on which they were working. The Kwik Fit guy was able to use a spare key he had and fitted a new tyre. Job done, first day of the holiday another £70 down the drain.

Before we went away, I looked up on Google local villages, pubs and craft beers. I made a list of three, and over the time we were in Weymouth, we went to some very pretty villages and had some really good ales. On one occasion, we had a couple of sandwiches. They were good value with salad, chips and were well filled for £7.95. When I came to pay, the guy fiddled with his till and asked for £25. I said £7.95 twice in my book was £15.90. I apologised for doing it in my head but that was the price of two sandwiches. He went away to ask for instruction and came back and said he would take

£15.90. I am dumbfounded by the stupidity of some of the recently educated morons of society.

12th February

It has been unseasonably warm of late, but today, it has turned very cold. We are very lucky in that our house backs onto Mewsbrook Park and Lake. Every day, many people jog, walk, jiggle or take their dogs there. We can always tell when it turns cold because when a dog squats and craps, there are four of five people who rush over with black poo bags to collect the steaming stuff to keep their hands warm!

In case you're wondering what jigglers are. They are lady joggers who don't wear sports bras.

14th February

Gill and I went out for a walk and thought we would have some lunch. I suggested going to the Rustington Manor Hotel. It is a series of about four houses converted into a hotel. It always looks nice when I walk past and has a menu displayed on a board outside and welcomes, 'non-residents'. It was just after 12.30 when I pushed the front door. It would not open so I pushed the bell. A guy came to the door and apologised for the door being locked. I said we would like to come in for lunch. "Sorry, we are closed. We only are open Fridays, Saturdays and Sundays." Hello, this is a hotel. Only open at the weekends! Disgusted and hungry, we walked away and finished up at L'Establo for lunch.

25th February

We have had a few days away in Bournemouth. Our usual friendly travel company sent us a letter offering a five-day break, half board with evening entertainment for £69. We had to go. Had a good time and one night we tied in the quiz. Gill and I played as a team and two other teams of about six or seven people tied with us so there was a tie break question. "How many people have been killed by cows from 2001–2019?" I said six. Way out! The right answer was 73!

1st March

My daughter came to visit last weekend, and I showed her a clothes catalogue I have been using. I asked if she wanted anything from it, and she chose a pair of trousers. I ordered them, and they arrived by post a few days later. Today, I went to the post office with a parcel to send. I put the parcel on the weighing machine and said to the lady behind the counter, "First class inland please." She asked what was in it and how much is it worth? I told her they were trousers and worth about £30. She said that the postage would be £14.75. I was gobsmacked, £14.75! I expressed a modicum of surprise. She said that was the price for anything over £20 in value. "Oh, I remember," I said, "I bought them in a sale for £10. How much now?" She said it was something like £10. I could not believe it, but they were for my daughter so I said okay. She passed me through a customs leaflet to fill out. Alarm bells went off in my head, Sutton was, by my last recollection, in Surrey, part of the United Kingdom…I filled out the form and slipped it back to the lady. She asked me to give her the parcel. I did and she printed off a label to put on the parcel. "This is going to Sutton," she said. "I thought you said it was going to New Zealand." Pennies dropped, that's why it was £14 plus. She charged me for the parcel going to New Zealand. How 'first class inland please' came out as New Zealand, I shall never know. Bottom line, she charged me £3 odd for the postage, and I departed.

4th March

We have a bird feeder in the garden. We do not have a squirrel feeder. This has obviously not been understood by the family of squirrels living at the bottom of our garden. Wherever I positioned the bird feeder, the squirrels always managed to get to it. I found a five-foot long metal bar from somewhere in the garden and drilled a small hole through the trunk of a tree, slipped the bar through the hole and hung the bird feeder from the extended bar. The squirrels managed to walk along the bar, hang upside down and access the bird feeder. I bought a box of fence spikes that you put along the top of fences to stop birds and other pest alighting on the fence. I tied two of these along the metal bar. The squirrels obviously belong to a sadist S&M club as they were still able to walk along the spikes, hang upside down and eat the bird seed. I decided to get a plastic flower pot, put a hole through its bottom and hang it upside down, put a piece of string through the hole and attach the bird feeder to the string. My thoughts being that squirrels could not grip onto the plastic flower pot and get to the bird seed. So far this seems to be working.

5th March

Oh, no, it's not! We saw the little sod this morning gripping by its toenails on the bottom lip of the flower pot hanging full length upside down and getting to the bird seed. I have now lengthened the string through the flower pot so the seed holder is further down and surely further away than the length of the squirrel's body.

7th March

Squirrels can jump quite high! Today, they were standing on the grass and jumping up to catch onto the bird feeder. I have now put wire through the bird feeder and down through another upturned flower pot. My thoughts are now that they will have nothing to grab onto if they jump up. The flower pot is perhaps four inches wide. So, we have an arrangement where a long metal bar is extended from the tree from which a wire hangs. This goes through the base of an upturned plastic flower pot and that wire continues down to the bird feeder. Another wire goes from the bird feeder down through another, smaller flower pot. Let's see if this works.

8th March

Over the past five days, I have received four telephone calls from people pretending to represent BT Openreach and saying my internet is compromised and I need to listen to their instruction and act accordingly...As if!

I went along with the first one for a while. He asked me to press the key with the Microsoft logo on it then press R. I apologised and said, "Sorry what was that key to press?"

"R, R for Roger."

"My name is Geoffrey, not Roger, why would I press R for Roger when I am Geoffrey?" He soon gave up and put the phone down. Another couple of calls came and went then I was obviously in the mood for banter when another call came in. Same scenario, my internet was compromised could I etc., etc., etc. I said, "Can you hold on please? I am having sex with my partner. I'll be a while; can you hold or will you give me your phone number and I'll call you later?" Phone went dead. I have not had a call since.

12th March

Went to the Spotted Cow for a drink at lunchtime. Richard was there and as usual, engaged us in conversation. He is a mad keen Liverpool supporter and had bought a new Liverpool scarf. It shows all the European cups they have won, where they won them and the dates. Very nice if you are a Liverpool supporter, but I really couldn't give a toss. He went on to say that today was his mother and father's wedding anniversary. Sixty-six years he said. That sounded impressive. Then with a straight face, he said that his dad had walked out on the family when he was 11 and he never saw him again. It was two years after he died that Richard and his sister were made aware their father was dead.

14th March

A virus named Corona Virus 19 has spread from China. It is serious in the way that most people may catch it. Warnings and advice are that we must wash hands and be careful not to spread the virus.

15th March

This is getting very serious now. They are talking of isolating older people who are more liable to get the virus.

16th March

How about this...All football, rugby and public gatherings cancelled. Lots of talk going on about business failures. The world is beginning to panic.

17th March

Shop shelves are being stripped bare with people hoarding food and essentials. Toilet rolls seem to be a big thing. From my understanding, this virus does not give you the shits. It is a sore throat and cough. Talk of schools shutting and travel restrictions.

18th March

Yes, schools are shutting, all public gatherings stopped. Pubs, restaurants and cinemas, theatres, etc. being closed. People are being laid off work. Business telling people to work from home, don't travel. Airlines and hotels in a panic.

19th March

Exams cancelled in schools. Schools may not reopen until September! The football season has been postponed and discussions are underway as to how to proceed. Call an end to the season...Current leaders named Champions bottom three relegated? The legal implications are huge. Television companies have bought the rights to many live sporting events. There are none! Everything is cancelled. The Olympics are in doubt for the coming June. Wimbledon is in doubt and the cricket season on hold. This is taking a crisis too far. People are dying of this virus worldwide. But the numbers include many who were seriously ill with respiratory problems anyway. The numbers of people who die each day from TB, HIV/AIDS, malaria, pneumonia far, far outstrip those who die of this virus. Yet the world has gone nuts. Cities are closed down, inter country travel is almost at a standstill. Businesses are crippled. People being laid off. The government has pledged a limitless amount of money to fund those in need.

Those over 70 are at most risk. We are told to self-isolate. Don't go out. This is total madness.

When walking home from buying my newspaper, I saw a white van parked by the road with the sign, 'No toilet rolls stored in this van overnight'. Priceless.

23rd March

The prime minister last night addressed the nation and declared a state of emergency. All non-essential shops are to close; people are not allowed on the street unless to buy essential food. Police can invoke fines for people going out without good reason. The country is in lockdown.

All gatherings banned; Olympics cancelled.

26th March

My daily paper has offered free delivery of newspapers. Given the restrictions and advice not to go outdoors unless to buy essential food. I thought I'd take advantage of this free delivery of newspapers. Today, my coupons arrived. I have six coupons, one for each week. Six in all. Fine. The accompanying letter says I am to give these coupons to my local participating newsagent and arrange with them for payment of the newspapers. No problem I thought. Then I looked at my given local newsagent. They are in Little Chalfont. Little Chalfont I think is in Buckinghamshire and certainly over 80 miles from Littlehampton where I live (I looked on the atlas). Where are the Candid Camera cameras? This is bloody mad. So, I telephoned the number given as shown on the letter and explained to the lady that their suggested delivery newsagent was over 80 miles away and that given self-isolation, I would prefer not to drive for three plus hours to get to the shop and for the owner to tell me he does not deliver to Littlehampton. She offered another vendor who happens to be about a mile away. Okay, I could live with this. I made a note of their name and address, thinking, I'll go over tomorrow and arrange payment for the papers. I then looked more closely at the six vouchers. They are individually dated. One voucher per week. So far so good. However, the first week is the last week of July and the last, sixth week, is the last week in August…We are in late March!

27th March

A couple of days ago, having mown my back lawn and with nothing else to do for the next nine months of lockdown, I decided to also mow the front grass outside my house. There are areas of maybe 20 ft by 50 ft outside each house along the road. The council mow these strips of grass maybe three times a year; I and some of my neighbours do like to keep the front of our houses looking as nice as possible, and we do mow the grass outside our respective houses reasonably regularly. Today, the council were out mowing the common areas. They went along the road cutting everyone's front grass but mine! I saw him cut next door's then he went out into the road, missed my bit and went on down the road! I pay bloody Council Tax to include this service, and I am discriminated against because I choose to prefer my house looking as nice as I can.

Our house overlooks a park. In that park is a children's playground. Yesterday, the council decided to close the playground, presumably because the virus could attach itself to the swings, slides, roundabouts, etc. and the kids could pick up the virus. Yesterday, two blokes fixed warning signs up on the gates and put yellow and black tape across the gates barring entry. Today, I was having lunch and happened to look out the window to see a guy lift his child, who was about six or seven, over the fence and into the playground. What an utter twerp!

4th April

Yesterday was Gill's daughter Wendy's birthday. Tomorrow is Gill's 70th. For several months now, we have arranged to hold a family party today to celebrate both events. Of course, it has been cancelled due to the current events and lockdown. Gill is devastated. Very tearful but there is nothing anyone can do. The local Chinese restaurant is not taking delivery orders so we arranged for a delivery from the Indian.

6ᵗʰ April

Still in lockdown, not allowed to socialise at all. Number of deaths rising. Prime Minister Boris Johnson was taken into intensive care two days ago and is still there. We and most of our friends have stopped looking at the news on television. It is all about the virus, what to do, what not to do. It is all doom and gloom, so we don't bother watching it anymore.

Several months ago, the continuing rains led to some rivers flooding and many, many peoples' houses were flooded and fields under water. Not a word has been said about them. The fields are now pretty much dry as we have had no rain for a couple of weeks. I do find it curious that the victims of flooding seem to have been overlooked.

8ᵗʰ April

I was reading the newspaper this morning when Gill commented I was reading it from the front to back. Yes, that's right! Forever, as long as I can remember, I read the paper back to front. Sport first then the financial reports, then the other stuff. There is no sport and the financial pages are all full of doom and gloom with the stock market tanked and the financial pages full of the virus and its effects on business.

11ᵗʰ April

Gill is still so depressed following the cancellation of her birthday party. She has swollen glands, a sore throat and cough. I think she is picking up bugs by being so 'low'.

21st April

Into the fourth week of lockdown and there is little sign things are getting back to normal. My dentist phoned this morning referencing my six-monthly check-up due on 7th May. They need to postpone it and rescheduled for 7th September. Dentists are closed and not seen as essential to life!

22nd April

I walked to our local Tesco Express shop to buy a newspaper. I was about third in line of a queue of about eight outside the shop, when the lady in charge of limiting customer access to the shop said, "Oh, how cute, you're so sweet, so lovely."

"Thank you," I said.

"No, not you, I was talking about the little dog behind you." So much for my ego!

23rd April

I walked into Rustington this morning, partly for exercise, partly to buy some milk and bread. Rustington is about a fifteen-minute walk. By the time I got there, my bowels were telling me I should have gone to the toilet before I left home. There is a public toilet next to the church, which I arrived at just in time. A notice outside said, 'Due to the Corona virus 19 lockdown, this facility is closed until further notice…In emergency, call 07987356112.' I wondered just what sort of emergency other than the one I found myself would justify ringing the number. My return home took about ten minutes due to my very good impression of Monsieur Poirot's walk.

24ᵗʰ April

Hairdressing salons are closed as part of the general lockdown. My hair is now at late 1960s/70s lengths. Well, over my collar almost resting on my shoulders.

3ʳᵈ May

Each day, we eat breakfast, dinner and often lunch at our dining table overlooking Mewsbrook Park. The regular dog walkers, joggers, jigglers and pleasure walkers pass by each having their own routine and regularity. Over the time, we have given certain of those regular's names. Mr Lesser spotty, a man with a Dalmatian with fewer spots than I would have thought normal. Mr Two tone, a guy who wears pink shorts and an orange top. Mrs Sausage, a lady with a sausage dog. Mr and Mrs Scotty, an elderly couple with two white West Highland Terriers. Mr and Mrs Scotty are very regular; she has a walking stick, and they must be in their 80s. The two dogs are always on leads. Rarely, maybe once a fortnight Mr Scotty is on his own. Mrs Scotty not with him. We have noticed recently that when Mr Scotty is on his own, he will take the two dogs off the lead and let them play. They love it. They run around, chasing each other having a great time. Strange though when Mrs Scotty is around, they are always on the lead. Today, Mr Scotty was on his own and let the dogs off. They were running around having a ball, then, about five minutes later, we saw a lady striding across the grass waving her stick in the air. We at first thought the lady was acknowledging someone she knew. No, this was Mrs Scotty striding across the grass brandishing her stick at her husband. Poor man bent down called the two dogs who immediately came to him and he tethered them on leads. I hope he had had his breakfast before coming out as he was surely in her bad books.

8th May

Another day in lockdown. They say things may be allowed to open up a little next week; we are awaiting a statement from the government on Sunday. Hopefully, playgrounds, garden centres and other open spaces will be allowed to open.

Having been to the chemist to collect my pills and done some essential shopping, such as three bottles of wine, I was confronted, as I arrived home, by a neighbour who said, "Let's get together and have a street party at 3.30 ish this afternoon." Sounded good to me. It is the 75th anniversary of VE Day. Why not?

It is a beautiful day. Given the restrictions of lockdown, I was surprised, pleased and amazed that everyone on the close attended. There are eight houses in our cul-de-sac. We have lived here three years and know and spoken to people in maybe five of the eight houses. We gathered at the end of the road, everyone bringing their own chairs and drink and everyone from every house attended. Maybe it is a sign of the times that people miss the personal social interaction, but everyone was there. We passed an enjoyable two and a half hours and promised 'we should do this again' soon.

Just finished dinner. I cooked a stir fry, had some garlic bread and of course a glass of wine. I went out onto the balcony overlooking the park and lake and thought, *you know, I don't think I have been happier in my life.* The scene was beautiful in the early evening sun. I had had a nice dinner and a lovely afternoon. I felt life was good. Really good.

10th May

Gill is de-frosting the fridge-freezer. We have been eating our way through the freezer bits for a while and not replacing them. Essential to finish off the rose and white wine before they get too warm.

22nd May

Where does the time go?

There is talk about loosening up the lockdown regulations and children being allowed back to school. The unions are up in arms that teachers will be put at risk! There are 22 other European countries where schools have re-opened, union bigwigs are quoted as calling young children they teach 'snot ridden' and other derogatory terms.

I went shopping today, needed various bits and wanted to go to the garden centre now they are allowed to open and get a few bedding plants. After the garden centre, I went to Asda. Parked and walked towards the queue. NO WAY. I turned around, got into my car and left. Next stop Sainsbury. I drove into the car park and decided not to park but drive around to see how far the queue stretched. Drove out again! I thought I would go to Tesco. While on my way I realised I would pass Morrisons so decided to pull in and see if their queue was shorter. It was. In fact, they had two queues, one for basket shoppers and one for trolley shoppers. I thought this was a good idea. However, basket in hand and a shopping list containing milk, beer, wine, lemonade, Coca Cola, bread, laundry bubbles and a bottle of Pimms, I was loaded down quite quickly. When I got home and unpacked the purchases, I found one of the eight-pack Coca Cola cans had been punctured and there was no coke in it, but the tab was still secure. I was not about to go all the way back to Morrisons and complain but thought it worth a mention.

24th May

Some lockdown restrictions are being eased but still most shops closed. Some schools will open next week for one or two years. Not everyone.

27th May

Some parents are threatening to sue the government for stopping their children going to school over the past several weeks. Others are threatening to sue the government for forcing their children back to school soon.

McDonalds open drive through and take away. Queues are said to be a mile long. Pictures in the newspaper shows cars nose to tail...To buy a coffee or hamburger! These must be the same parents 'see above'!

28th May

On a walk around the lake today, I noticed the family of swans have seven goslings and a family of ducks have also seven ducklings. The moorhens have a brood of four. Over the recent days, we have seen other baby birds, squirrels and a fox. It's all going on.

1ˢᵗ June

Now allowed to congregate in groups of six and visit other people's homes but only their gardens and stay two metres apart. I went for a walk along the beach. It was very busy. I saw a crowd of girls in their bikinis and swimsuits. I had to walk past five or six times to make sure I counted correctly. There were nine and not keeping two metres apart. Let me walk past again. Yes, nine of them.

Horse racing started behind closed doors. Football due to restart in a couple of weeks again behind closed doors and on neutral grounds.

2ⁿᵈ June

A seagull has been nesting on our roof. Wedged between the roof and chimney. They have been sitting on the nest for weeks but no sign of a baby. I did see a broken egg shell on the balcony.

3ʳᵈ June

It has started to rain. Very light but it is rain. This is the first for a long time. They say May was the sunniest month 'ever' on record.

6th June

It is rather cloudy today but felt the need to get out for a walk. We went around Swanmore Lake in Arundel. It is very pretty. There were a number of other people walking around the lake some overtly social distancing, others could not give a toss. We saw a couple coming towards us, and the lady appeared to be holding sweater under her arm; as we got closer, no, it wasn't a sweater; it was a parrot! Yes, a parrot. A white parrot with green comb, I think that's what they are called. We walked on stunned. Stopped, looked at each other. "She was taking her parrot for a walk," I said to Gill. "Got to get home and commit this to my memoirs." On our way out of the lake, we were on the road walking towards our car when we saw the bird lady approach us again. They had walked the opposite way around the lake and had finished at the same time as us and was on the road as well. As we passed them, the parrot spoke. "Hello," it said. Gill and I were in a fit of giggles until we reached our car.

7th June

Saw two baby seagulls today on the roof. Obviously hatched overnight. Hope, they don't fall off the roof!

10th June

Pandemonium broke out last night just after midnight. It seems a fox got onto our roof and took the two seagull chicks. An almighty row.

11th June

We drove up to my son Simon's house in Surrey. We went on the M23 and past the usual signs, roadworks, narrow lanes, average speed limit. Then we came across a sign that said, 'Beware Danger Covid Virus'. I was expecting some caped villain to jump out of the bushes and attack the car!

24th June

We are being told that the two-metre distancing is to be reduced to one metre and schools will be closed until September. Theatres can open but with no live performances …Hello!

Gyms, swimming pools and clubs to stay shut. Hairdressers, pubs and restaurants can open but with social distancing rules. You have to 'book in' to a pub, give them your name and phone number and pay by a phone app. What the hell is a phone app? I have a landline telephone at home that has served me well for fifty plus years. I don't have a mobile phone, and I am not going to get one. I don't see how this is going to work, but I will be at the Spotted Cow on Sunday morning to chance my arm.

26th June

The past few days have been very hot and beaches have been packed. Some areas have been gridlocked with people. Social distancing?

Pubs and restaurants are to be allowed to open from 4th July. I hear that to conform to social distancing requirements, we will need to register with the pub owner, giving them our names and phone numbers. This is so we can be traced if someone, somewhere contacts Covid-19 and they have visited the pub. We need to register our attendance, prebook our drinks, pay for them on an APP, whatever that is. It occurs to me you can rub shoulders with strangers when you march in protests and riot, spit and yell in the faces of policemen, lie buttock to buttock on a beach next to people you don't know, leave behind tons of germ and virus infested litter for others to pick up, yet you have to register to go to the pub; you cannot sing in church and you must wear a mask when on a bus. Apart from the driver, you are probably the only person on the bus anyway!

5th July

The parks and playgrounds opened yesterday. Today after a rainy start is sunny but windy and the playground in Mewsbrook Park is crowded with young children. We are told schools will only return in September. Our school kids will have had six months off since March by the time they go back to school in September yet they can run around in playgrounds but are not allowed back to school. Teachers I see are getting up to £95 an hour giving tutorials online yet protest it is dangerous for them to go back to school. Are they going to disclose this £95 an hour earnings for tax as well as getting their furloughed salary? It seems inequitable to me that they say that going into school to teach is dangerous for them. Kids are supposed to be the least susceptible to this virus. Once again, it is the few with the loudest voices that seem to dictate how the rest of us live.

11th July

Week umpteen of the lockdown and more and more businesses are opening. There are more people on the roads and in shops. We went to a major Tesco store today and did not need to queue; we walked straight in. Five weeks ago, we would have queued twenty or thirty minutes to get in.

The newspapers have recently shown pictures of crowded beaches and beauty spots and the litter left behind after everyone has gone home. It is sickening to see the amount of rubbish left behind. How difficult is it to take home the stuff you brought with you? I think it would be a great idea if the Bournemouth Council established an open-air museum dedicated to 'Rubbish of the Twenty-First Century'. They could use the seven-mile stretch of beach, promenade and surrounding roads. Parking may be difficult and donations discouraged. However, contrary to other museums, visitors would be encouraged to steal and take home exhibits!

14th July

For some weeks now, travellers on public transport have had to wear masks. Despite there may be only one customer, they must wear a mask, but the driver does not! The government are now saying from next week anyone going into a shop must wear a mask. But staff in the shop do not have to wear masks. Is this absolutely nuts? We can go into pubs and drink, we can go into restaurants to eat, yet going into a shop, we must now wear a mask. We are told we cannot touch produce in shops unless we are buying them. Tell me a woman that does not go up to a dress or whatever she is buying and have a feel and a touch of the material. It's the same with books. You can't pick them up unless you buy them. How about in restaurants and cafes? Are you allowed to touch the menus, knives and forks? Are you allowed to drink from the cups? This is blooming madness. We have been in lockdown for several months. Many people have chosen to wear masks. But now as life is slowly coming out of lockdown with people now able to socialise in small groups and with their families, etc., one would think this loosening of regulation should not trigger the compulsion for shoppers now to wear masks. There will be fines enforced.

When going into a pub or restaurant, we are asked our names and telephone numbers. If we go into other shops or go onto the beach or park, no one asks our names and phone numbers! Can you imagine a bloke going up to a young lady on the beach, she is almost wearing a bikini and the bloke asks for her name and phone number? "Just doing my social duty in case I get Covid-19." What tosh. How many ways is that politically incorrect? This society has gone mad.

16th July

Another stupidity! Russell, Gill's daughter Wendy's partner, was sent home from work with a sore throat. He was told not to return to work until he had had a Corona Virus check-up. He went online to see where the nearest testing station was and found one in Midhurst some 15 miles away. He drove there and was denied access as it was military camp and for military personnel only! Fifteen-mile journey home. He then found the next closest testing station was in Portsmouth 25 miles away. Is this crazy or what?

17ᵗʰ July

My car went in for an MOT yesterday. I went to the garage this morning to collect it. It would not start. I went back to reception and got a chap with a booster battery to jumpstart the car. I had never had a problem starting the car, but he said that they had found the battery was flat that morning. Had they left a door open all night? Who knows? Bottom line, the battery was flat. The chap suggested I took the car for a run before I went home. This I did. I went on a twenty-minute run and went home.

18ᵗʰ July

Car didn't start. I called out the 'Home Start' people and the guy said the battery was too flat to test if it was holding a charge. The battery was more than eight years old so maybe it was dead. Having started the car, I drove over to Halfords for them to test the battery and see if I need a new one. Of course, I did! The guy fitted a new one and reprogrammed my digital radio; obviously, when the battery was taken out, all electrical stuff was cut off; £107 later, I drove out of Halfords with a new battery. I noticed a red frost warning light on my dashboard. It's the third week of July. It must be 20 degrees outside; how can the frost warning light be on? I studied the dashboard, and there was the answer. My outside temperature reading was minus 67 degrees F. Yes, okay, that's frosty! I noticed too that the digital clock showed the time to be about ten minutes slow. Fair enough. Battery disconnected, etc., etc. I thought I'd reprogramme the clock when I got home.

I am not too savvy with technology, but I had reset the clock several times since I had the car, twice a year when the clocks change. Oh...the year said 2003. I tried to reset the year, but it looped through 2003 to 2013 then back to 2003. After two or three tries, I got the hump. The temperature was wrong too showing a minus figure in Fahrenheit. I thought the temperature was an ambient fact, not something I could adjust. Scrolling through, I found temperature on the computer and pressed a button a few times. Nothing happened. Then gave up. I grabbed the owner's manual and went in doors for a cup of coffee. A couple of hours later, I thought I'd have another try. I went into 'Menu' and saw something that said metric and something else. I fiddled and diddled about, not quite knowing what I was doing, pressed a few more buttons, saw it was still anytime between 2003 and 2013 and went indoors.

19th July

Gill has gone to a friend's house in Selsey. She won't be back for lunch so I went to the pub. Temperature gauge is correct 20 degrees C! It is still 2013. By the time I got to the pub, I realised I had travelled 5.3 km. I've been travelling in miles ever since I passed my test, and now, I am travelling in kilograms or whatever they are called. I remembered that when fiddling with the menu, I came across the word metric. I thought I may have pressed that and it altered my settings. Sure enough, a swift reprogramming (I am getting the hang of this), and I am back in miles. It occurred to me that having pushed the metric button by mistake, if I put the radio on, it may come out in French. I switched on Smooth FM, and thank goodness, Womack and Womack sang out in English. Went into the pub and had lunch. It is still 2013, by the way. I decided to change it to 2010 thinking it would wind me up a little less than being at 2013.

20ᵗʰ July

My children have been on at me to 'come into the twentieth century'. They think I am a bit of a Luddite when it comes to technology. I refuse to have a mobility phone. I have a landline and a computer that does e-mail. I am happy with that. The only two phone calls I make are to the Indian and Chinese takeaways. The last two phone calls I remember receiving were from my dentist in May telling me my six-monthly check-up had been delayed because of Covid-19 to September and the other day from the garage telling me my car was ready to collect. I do not need to pay out shed loads of money on a mobility phone when I have a landline. Anyway, I reminded my kids, we were in the twenty-first century not the twentieth. "No, Dad, you are so far behind you need to get as far as the twentieth century, then you can see how it goes." I paid good money for their education and this is how they treat me.

22ⁿᵈ July

When we are eating our meals, we can see across the park and into a children's playground. There are routine dog walkers, joggers, jigglers, cyclists. Also, the Arun Council men who check the playground equipment, empty the rubbish bins and cut the grass. Once a week on a Wednesday, the dog poo man comes with his yellow bag. The rubbish men have black bin liners, the dog poo man has yellow. Last week, two men came to change the bin. I thought this was a bit over the top, but there again, I thought the second chap maybe a trainee learning the route the location of the dog poo bins in various streets and parks. Today, again two men arrived. I mentioned to Gill that perhaps this trainee was a slow learner. "Maybe he is a security guard," she said. I thought this was very probable. Obviously, dog poo has an intrinsic value and needs guarding whereas common rubbish can be collected by one man.

A thought then struck me. Over the past couple of weeks since guidelines over social distancing had been loosened, the park has been packed most days. Crowds of children and adults walking, sitting and playing together instead of being in school or in work. I bet someone has lost an engagement ring and thought they saw a dog swallow it. I reckon they have written to Arun Council and asked that dog poo in Mewsbrook Park be collected and analysed under strict security to see if the ring can be discovered.

It is still 2010.

24th July

As of today, it is a requirement that all shoppers wear face nappies when entering shops. Staff in those shops do not need to wear them! I am grasping to find the scientific logic behind this. Shop workers I have spoken to say wearing a face nappy all day would be too hot, would facilitate acne and face irritation.

4th August

Over the past few days, there has been an uptick in the number of Covid-19 cases especially in the Midlands.

Leicester, Blackburn, Oldham. This is just as the rest of the country is trying to loosen up and get back to work. There is a strong suggestion schools will reopen in September. I note that some experts in the education sector say that opening the schools is essential and pubs may need to shut to compensate! Hello…Where is the logic in this? Is underage drinking of such endemic proportions that if 5–17 years olds go back to school, there will be no custom in pubs forcing them to close?

I am told by a friend who works in the retail sector that customer returns to the shop are isolated for 72 hours before being put back on the shelves. However, new products delivered from suppliers are loaded immediately onto shelf for sale. Double standards or what?

21st August

I saw a young chap today riding his bike in the park. He was probably late teens, early twenties. He had passed at least two 'no cycling' signs. He was not wearing a helmet, was not holding the handlebars but was using both hands to fiddle on his electronic gadget. He was also wearing a face nappy. Is there double standards here about health and safety?

24th August

I have my diabetes check-up next week. Delayed by three months due to this virus that is destroying our society, economy and lives. I need to bring a urine sample, so I went to the surgery to collect a sample jar. The doors are locked and one must ring for attention. Did so and was promptly answered by a masked assistant. "May I have a urine sample bottle, please?" I asked. She went away and came back within seconds and at chest height, arms-length offered me a sample jar. "Can you lower your arms, please?" I asked. She burst out laughing and said I could have the bottle for free as I had a great sense of humour. They usually cost 20p so that was a result.

31ˢᵗ August

Many people have been working from home now for months. There is an ongoing debate as to if the 'norm' of working from an office will ever return. London is very, very quiet. Local restaurants, sandwich bars, pubs, dry cleaners, all sorts of ancillary shops are closing as there is no one about. People are saying they would rather work from home. It saves time and money not to commute. If people are refusing to 'go back to work in an office', does it not beg the question: will their employers reduce their salaries by the London Weighting allowance all these people have added to their salary to work in London? Does it also raise the possibility that people working from home in Mumbai or Karachi can equally do the job of someone working from home in suburbia and do it for a quarter of the cost? Would that not help the economy by reducing employers' overheads?

1ˢᵗ September

We had dinner at the Black Rabbit last night. It was the last day of the dine out deal introduced by the government for the month of August. We have taken advantage of the offer a number of times during the month. It occurs to me the huge success of this programme has encouraged many, many people to eat out at pubs and restaurants. I wonder how many of these folk will now go back to work in their offices with proper segregation, sanitation and social distancing?

4th September

I had an appointment this morning at the doctors to see the nurse and give a blood sample as part of my diabetes check-up. As is now the requirement, I arrived five minutes before my appointment wearing a face nappy. I rang the bell by the locked front door and was quickly answered by a young lady that instructed me to use the sanitary gel. She pointed me to a notice on the door which asked if I have suffered from a cough, high temperature, had been diagnosed with etc., etc. I said that I had a cough and a high temperature when I was about 11 or 12 years old. She asked me to come in and stand 'in the box'.

She checked my details and told me to wait in the waiting room. Five minutes after my appointment time, I was called into a small room by the nurse. I had brought with me, as requested, a urine sample and a completed questionnaire. After checking my name and date of birth, she asked for the urine sample. I mentioned that my dog Max was unwell and I, this morning, had taken his urine sample to the vet. I was unsure if I had mistakenly switched the samples. She gave me two new sample jars 'in case they needed a new sample'.

I hear that more people are coming into the UK by rubber dinghy across the channel than via Heathrow.

10th September

New restrictions in place from tomorrow limiting social gatherings to six people. This is all due to a sudden spike in people being tested positive for the virus. Interestingly, the vast majority are 20–35-year-olds. These are some of the least likely people to die from it, but they can of course infect older relatives. We suffer for the stupidity of the young. These young idiots think they are immortal going to mass raves and parades. I hope the police will enforce the fines that are being introduced for breeches of these new restrictions.

28th September

Life is opening up a little more. The bowls club has reopened but with a maximum of six players to a rink and the club will use every other rink.

1st October

Went to a wine tasting at our local pub. Gill is not a big drinker and prefers rose wine. I am very happy to drink rose, white or red as long as there is plenty of it. The guy offered me a glass of 'something light and sparkling'. I said that was probably more to Gill's taste. He asked my preference and I said, "Something heavy, full bodied, dense and cheap, like my women." I got an almighty thump on my shoulder. Gill heard me.

8th November

Following another uptick in people testing positive for the virus and hospital admissions rising, we are again in lockdown mark 2. Pubs, restaurants and all non-essential businesses closed. The government has extended through to March the scheme where they pay up to 80% of employees' salary. This is madness. The actual death toll from the virus is minimal. Deaths due to cancer, stroke, heart disease are on the rise due to lack of care for these folks as medical attention is focussed on the virus. If you test positive for the virus yet die from a heart attack, the statistics show you died of Covid-19. Wrong, wrong, wrong. The new shut down regulations are different in different parts of the UK. Scotland, Wales, Ireland has their own regulations. How about this, in Wales you cannot buy female sanitary products or baby milk formulae, but you can buy alcohol from supermarkets. Lockdown stipulates you can sleep with your partner, but you cannot play bowls with them. Pubs and restaurants where you need to give your name and contact details while seated at segregated tables are closed; yet you can walk in the park and High Street, go to supermarkets shoulder to shoulder with strangers.

You can take your dog to the vet, but you cannot see your doctor.

Life has become crazy.

4th December

Yes, another long time since my last rant. This is the time of year when people send Christmas cards. Over the past few years, e-mail cards have become popular as the cost of buying and sending traditional cards has risen astronomically. According to latest scientific advice, the use of e-mail and the internet is more polluting and an enhancement to climate change than sending postal mail! All I can say is that I am glad I am not as clever as these experts. Their brains must be so frazzled in deducing that paper/cards, envelopes, stamps, the labour and cost and pollution involved in the collecting, sorting and onward delivery of mail is somehow less polluting than sending an e-mail.

At this time, a new type of lockdown has been implemented. There are three tiers of lockdown and related laws. Most of us are locked into Tier 2 and the social implications that brings. We can go shopping, rubbing shoulders with all and sundry, walking in aisles that are too narrow, queuing at checkout points that are too few, so queues lead back into the already crowded aisles. Yet, I cannot go to the pub, sign in my name and contact details, sit at a sanitised table socially distanced from the next table and enjoy table service by staff of a pint of beer. I am required by law to have a 'substantial meal'. A substantial meal is open to local definition and varies from pub to pub. The top scientific experts have obviously decided that the Corona 19 virus can be caught by drinking alcohol alone but the antidote is to eat a meal. It has taken the experts since, what...March/April to come up with this idea. This is just at the same time as they found a vaccine. Maybe and I am only suggesting this, but perhaps the vaccine is in fact beef and three veg liquidised into a smoothie and injected into the bloodstream.

Social distancing. That's another anomaly. My neighbour has for the past three months had, on a daily basis, up to six builders and trades people in her house at any one time. She is having major refurbishment work done. However, I cannot invite her into my house for a coffee. Children in the park are playing on slides, swings, roundabouts and seesaws, having a great time. Has anyone told the Corona 19 virus not to attach itself to playground facilities? I understand children may be less susceptible to suffer from the effects of the virus, but does the virus understand that it is forbidden to transfer itself onto accompanying adults? Perhaps playgrounds are virus-free zones? Perhaps, instead of working from offices or from home, businesses should set up in playgrounds outdoors. They are apparently virus-free zones.

At least now, non-essential shops and services have re-opened. We will be able to go to the hairdresser, optician, dentist, podiatrist, take our dogs to grooming parlours and the vet. I just hope that we do not need to see a doctor!

21st December

About 10 days ago, a vaccine was introduced to combat the virus. It is being rolled out to the oldest people and those on the frontline NHS. Every day, we have new numbers shown to us of the numbers of new cases of the virus, the numbers of new deaths. The government has introduced a new 'Tier 4' for London and most of the South East as new cases have jumped, said to be due to a new strain of the virus. These rules are more draconian than Tier 3 in so far as all non-essential shops and businesses are closed, and you cannot socialise with any household and only meet with one person outdoors. You can still walk side by side up the aisles of supermarkets brushing shoulders with who knows who though.

I look forward to statistics being released in about a month's time showing current new cases and deaths. Will they show that the number of people over 80 who have had the vaccination and have died in the past month against those deaths occurring in under 50s who have not had the injection? Statistics can and are used by the people commissioning them to show exactly what they want to show.

I need to re-order my pills so this morning I phoned the doctor's surgery to ask for a repeat prescription. I phoned at a minute to 8.00 am to be told the surgery opens at 8.00 please call back. I did and redialled immediately. I was then told by a two-minute, twenty-second recorded statement that the waiting list on the phone lines were full. Please call later. I did straight away and was told, following the same two-minute, twenty-second message the same thing; the lines are full please call later. About three minutes later, I redialled, and after a different recorded message was told, I was number 15 in line. Twenty odd minutes later, I was answered by a receptionist. I asked to re-order my prescription and was told they did not accept repeats over the phone! The various recorded messages I had listened to over the past half an hour told me the surgery was closed; how busy they were, dial 111 for this, 999 for that. Doctors are not seeing patients, put your symptoms in writing and someone may get back to you over the internet. Nothing about prescriptions. I am now told that despite the surgery being closed, I need to go there and put my repeat prescription in a box outside the surgery. Why the hell did they not say that in the recorded message? It would have saved me time and unclogged their telephone lines; I am sure most of the people waiting on line are only waiting to renew their prescription.

We tend to avoid looking at the news on television these days as it has for ages been doom and gloom. Life is depressing enough without idiots in the media asking politicians stupid questions. The country is in the middle of a pandemic, which seems at the moment to be getting out of control as new variants appear. Scientists don't know how to stop it, and the government can only act in good faith upon receipt of advice from scientists. Schools have just broken up for Christmas; one television reporter has just asked the prime minister if he could guarantee schools will go back as scheduled after the Christmas and New Year break. The PM cannot guarantee anything of the sort. What a stupid question.

24ᵗʰ December

Christmas Eve and the total lockdown laws come into force on Boxing Day. Gill and I decided to go for a drink at the pub as there is no knowing when or indeed if the pub will reopen. We gave our names, contact details upon entry, were escorted to a table where we were given service. Yes, we needed to have a light lunch to justify getting an alcoholic drink. That is the rules, go with it. Gill said it felt like *The Last Supper*. Totally sanitised, socially distanced, very safe environment. How different from supermarkets and playgrounds where people are brushing shoulder to shoulder and touching all different things which may or may not be contaminated. How strange is life?

5ᵗʰ January

Some schools have reopened taking only those children whose parents work in the frontline occupations. Pizza delivery drivers, supermarket cash out clerks, etc. All other kids are swarming around playgrounds in all sorts of un-sanitised, un-regulated environments.

15th January

We are well into the new total lockdown. Higher death rates each day and tens of thousands in hospital. The NHS is said to be at breaking point. The newspaper still show crowds of students playing together while police give people fines for sitting on a bench. Temporary mortuaries are opening as funeral parlours are over-crowded with dead bodies.

16th January

Gill's camera is several years old, and she wanted to replace it. A couple of weeks ago, we did some research online and selected one she wanted. Argos were selling it so we went online to try and buy it. The camera was out of stock at the local Rustington store and the three next closest stores, so we decided to wait a while. I went online last night and found the camera was now in stock locally so I thought I would surprise her and buy it. I went to collect it this morning, brought it home and she was pleased with the purchase. She opened the box and started to read the instructions. Apparently, you need to buy a memory card. Nowhere in the online sales and promotional literature was any indication that if you bought the camera, it would not work.

That is in fact the reality. I have paid £89.99 for a camera that does not work unless I buy a memory card. There is no indication of where I can buy a memory card, no indication of how much a memory card will cost. This is outrageous, scandalous. Surely, it is against the Trades Description Act to promote and sell a product that of itself as sold, does not work! I tried to telephone the Sony Customer Support line only to find it is a Monday to Friday facility.

A piece in the paper today displayed the devastating news that 'prepared' carrots were unavailable in several supermarkets. Heaven forbid, the thought of washing and peeling a carrot. What is this world coming too?

18th January

Having slept on it, my rage and anger at the need to purchase a memory card for the camera has subsided. I reasoned that if you buy a car, they don't advertise that you need to put petrol in it. It is assumed you know. When Gill bought a new phone over Christmas, she need to buy a 'sim card' before it would work. I suppose I am so old fashioned that it did not occur to me that cameras don't come fully working. Years ago, when I last bought a camera I had to buy a roll of film; I suppose it follows I need something to make it take pictures. So today, I decided to go to investigate the purchase of a memory card. I went online to the Sony website and logged into their customer service section for 'Help'. The site asked me to pay £5 to get my question answered and maintain an ongoing help service. I was outraged. How come I am asked to pay £5 for product advice? I researched further and found a telephone number, which I called. It was a London number, and I was eventually answered after going through the robotic loops and being on hold. The young lady spoke poor English, but I explained that I wanted to purchase a memory card for a specific camera. Where do I buy it? How much will it cost? What specifically do I need to buy, what product code? She said she would send me a link which would answer all my questions. This she proceeded to do. She asked if I would mind completing a short survey after she finished, to show how I felt about the service Sony provided. Oh, yes, you bet. I was patched through to a robotic survey the first question of which was, "How would you rate the overall experience of dealing with Sony on a scale of 1–10?"

I responded with, "One."

"Sorry, we do not understand your answer. How would you rate your overall experience of dealing with Sony?"

"One," I said again as clearly as I could.

"Sorry, we do not—" I did not wait any longer to put the phone down. I read the three-page printout the lady e-mailed me. I was looking for clues as to where I could purchase a memory card, how much it would cost, what is the specification I need to use to order one. I am sufficiently clued up to know there is probably different sizes or different products compatible with different model cameras. Not on these pages. All it told me was that I needed a memory card and gave four different names and references enshrouded in technical gobbledegook that I did not understand. I decided to go to the Argos store and ask the man behind the bar. I know this is only Click and Collect but I can't click if I don't know what I want to click! I felt it was necessary to take the order confirmation with me showing the order number and product code. Five-minute drive, walk straight up to the counter and gave the man my order confirmation, told him I had collected the product two days ago and proceeded with my request of what memory card did I need for this camera and could I buy it from them; I understand it is Click and Collect only, but I need to understand exactly what I need to buy. The guy looked at me with a rather strange look on his face. "This order confirmation is for a five kg tub of pointing cement you have bought from B&Q." Floor, please open up and swallow me. This is a bad day.

25th January

Gill and I went out for a walk this morning, just around the lake. Having read recently about some policemen being overly zealous in issuing fines for people supposedly having picnics, we wondered if sucking a mint while walking could be construed as having an illegal picnic.

27th January

We have had camelias flowering in the garden for some weeks, but today, a couple of daffodils broke open. I have not seen daffodils this early before.

1st February

What a day this has been! Since the beginning of lockdown, our social diary has been blank. Each day is 'same old, same old'. Each morning, we wake up and say, "It's fourteen hours until bedtime." Such is life. Today is Monday and Mondays are the highlight of the week. The cleaning lady comes. Gill has to get up, shower, have breakfast, dress, hoover, clean, dust, polish and generally tidy up before the cleaning lady arrives. Later this morning, we had a delivery of logs for the log burner. The man delivered half a lorry load. I asked him if they were numbered specifically or could they be used in any random order. He looked at me as if I were mad and said they could be used randomly. Just then, the post lady arrived with the post containing three books I had ordered. We spoke. Heavens above, my neighbour then walked past taking his dog for a walk. We chatted. Today, we spoke with four human beings. Four people. Unbelievable. We are exhausted.

2nd February

Reliably told in the newspaper that January was the coldest January ever recorded. Tell that to the daffs in my garden. Thank heaven for global warming. If it wasn't for global warming, it would have been really cold!

3rd February

Some weeks ago, some time in December, residents of this road were given literature issued by the council to show that civil engineering works would take place from 4th January to 1st February. This would cause disruption in the road and apologies made. Fair enough, bring it on.

A civil engineering company were working in partnership with the utility company to undertake the works. (Names have been withheld to protect their share price). They arrived nice and early on 4th January. Since that time, the 'Dig it and fill it' Debating Society, as I have called them, have spent several weeks sitting in, up to eight vans and lorries on a daily basis, walking and talking, on their phones and leaning on shovels. Why do in 10 days what you could string out and get paid for in 30 plus days. The work remains unfinished and the guys in high viz jackets continue to this day to walk, talk, debate and sit in vans.

4th February

Gill had her Covid vaccination this morning. They gave her a certificate and a document showing all sorts of side effects. They don't warn you of the side effects before they stick a needle in you, do they? Apparently, she had the Pfizer vaccine. There are other vaccines available, but I suppose it depends on what the surgery holds is what they give you. Gill said the nurse told her she may feel her arm get a little stiff following the injection. "That's because it's the Pfizer vaccine," I said. Gill looked quizzically at me. "Pfizer make Viagra," I said. "It's bound to make it a little stiff."

5th February

Last year, we had seagulls nesting on the roof. They built a nest, between the pitch of the roof and a chimney. The nest has been unoccupied since last summer, and Gill wanted it removed. She suggested I got up the ladder onto the roof and removed it. This was in hope that seagulls or other flappy, feathery vermin would not come back this year and nest in it.

I am not good with heights. I was not impressed with this suggestion. In fact, I would say that this was the worst idea since Mrs Ark said to Noah, "It's only a few drops of rain, I'll hang the washing on the line." Two thirds of the way up the ladder, I became very religious; an executive decision was made to leave the nest where it was. Call a 'Man', whatever, but I am not going up that ladder.

6th February

With hotels closed and leisure travel banned, the options for a summer holiday are limited. Gill and I have discussed various alternatives and decided that a week in bedroom 3 and a week in the conservatory would be the best we could hope for this year.

14th February

It's Sunday today. The 14th is the day our monthly direct debit is transferred from our personal bank accounts into the joint household account at Santander. We transfer £800 a month and have done so for about four years. Gill went to Tesco to buy some bits and pieces, which came to just under £50. An hour or so after, she returned home; she had a text message from Santander telling her we had gone overdrawn with an unauthorised overdraft. I went online through the computer to check our account and saw we also had an e-mail advising of an unauthorised overdraft. I was online and tried to contact the help desk as I saw our account was still in credit and in any event the £800 transfer had not gone through. I went on to the new-fangled online help section onto which Santander directs you instead of telephoning the help desk. Supposedly, I am talking to 'Ami'. I typed my situation stating my account was in credit, an £800 transfer had not been made and yet I have been informed I have an unauthorised overdraft. "Sorry, I do not understand the question," was the reply. It was obvious I was not 'talking' to anyone; this was just smoke and mirrors, and I was in contact with a robot. I decided to make a telephone call and was eventually connected to a human being. I explained my situation and the person (I am not allowed to say man, am I?) said that as it was Sunday, my £800 credit would not go through until tomorrow. The Tesco debit would not go through until the following day, Tuesday. As a reasonable person, I asked him why I had received two messages that I was in the position of being in an unauthorised overdraft. I pointed out to the human being that he had just told me the debit would not go through until next Tuesday and my £800 credit would, by that time, have been made; so why on earth have I been told incorrect information and wasted my time? Apparently, it is an automatic reaction triggered by robots to issue such notices. Should the robot not be aware that money is to be credited by automatic transfer? A robot, is a robot, is a robot. It is programmed to do the routine function of a human being. It has been badly programmed so as to recognise only debits to the account and not credits. I am a reasonable person, but technology and robots are making my life a misery.

22nd February

I understand the majority of school leavers are asking the Job Centre to find them a job with a company called Furlough. They have heard they pay good money and all you do is stay at home and receive your wages.

25th February

We learn today that schools will return for most children on 8th March. This is part of the larger roadway plan to return life to normal by June. I believe schools will have a reduced curriculum due to ongoing changes in society. Apparently, English grammar and spelling will no longer be taught. People today do not write letters. All correspondence is done via e-mail using spell checks, so children no longer need to spell. The conjugation of verbs will no longer be necessary and punctuation is a thing of the past. Text speak has overtaken the Queen's English. Each sentence should start with the word 'So' and contain at least three 'Likes'.

History will no longer be taught as the vast majority of events over the past four hundred years have been declared, inappropriate, racist or just did not really happen. Statues, monuments and buildings dedicated to historic figures have been, and continue to be, taken down as they offend a minority of people.

Mathematics will no longer be taught as everyone these days has a calculator; so, who needs to know their tables, addition and subtraction.

Home economics will also be shelved as no one cooks anymore; we all order takeaways and phone Just Eat.

Another casualty of the education system is English literature. Poems such as *Baa Baa Black Sheep* have been banned as racist. The story of *Sleeping Beauty* has been banned as it contains sexual assault. The princess is kissed while sleeping by the prince and therefore cannot give her consent to be kissed. *The Grand Old Duke of York* has been banned as the ten thousand men did not have proper union representation to advise them of their rights before they were marched up hill and down again for no particular reason and with no reference to comfort breaks during this march. Georgie Porgy has also fallen foul of the snowflake brigade. He kissed the girls and made them cry. This again must constitute sexual assault. However, the second verse, "When the boys came out to play, he kissed them too as he was gay," was considered quite acceptable. Obviously, five- to eight-year-olds these days do need to embrace diverse sexuality. The Health and Safety people have had a field day complaining that Cinderella's use of glass slippers was inappropriate and hazardous.

26ᵗʰ February

By the look of the date line to reopen society, it seems I shall not be able to travel to Stonehenge for the solstice on 28ᵗʰ March. I would have liked to have been part of the ceremony to push the stones forward an hour to catch the rising sun. The stones are huge and take a lot of shifting, so they like as many volunteers as possible. The stones need to be changed twice a year to coincide with the change in clocks by an hour. The Druids are very nice. They look like Klu Klux Clan on Valium. They don't have burning crosses but share the same fashion consultant.

9ᵗʰ March

There is a growing movement in society towards what is known as 'wokeness'. It is now considered improper to refer to a man as a man or a woman as a woman. We are all people. Those learned people at Manchester University are frowning upon the use of the words 'mother' and 'father' on application forms. Should it not follow then that the very name of the university, Manchester, should be changed to Personchester University? I doubt the citizens of Manchester will be too pleased that the name of their city be changed to Personchester. Should the Isle of Man now become the Isle of People? The Isle of Wight is surely racist! Maybe it should be the Isle of Pretty Coloured Sand?

13th March

Schools went back last Monday so we shall soon be getting statistics as to how many teachers have died in the last week due to contacting Covid-19. There are so many dedicated and wonderful teachers who continue to work hard. Unfortunately, it seems there are those amongst them who continue to advocate for more time off while getting paid. Surely with all the time schools have been closed, they could have / should have designed a system of testing, sanitising and segregating children without now losing more education time.

15th March

Gill got really upset this morning; she wanted to empty the hoover, took out the dust bag and found we had no replacement bag. I said we had plenty of red wine, and there were two bottles of white in the fridge, but it didn't make her feel any better.

21st March

Lovely day today, sunny, light cloud and negligible breeze. The park is busy and the playground packed with children. I reckon there must be more germs, viruses and bacteria per square metre in that playground from unclean, un-sanitised, swings, slides, roundabouts and seesaws than any segregated, sanitised and regulated restaurant or pub. Ours is not to reason why, ours is but to conform or die!

22nd March

Another glorious day. The sky is solid blue, the sun has a definite warmth and there is little breeze. We decided to put the table and chairs back out onto the veranda. They had been stored over winter in the garage. Had lunch on the veranda; it was really nice, overlooking the lake and park. Mrs Swan is still sitting on her eggs. The last of last year's brood left the lake a week or so ago to seek their own territory.

Newspapers are reporting scenes of violence. What had started out to be a peaceful demonstration against giving the police greater powers, hard core extremists triggered mass violence and rioting. Looking at pictures of thousands of people demonstrating led me to question their social distancing ethic. The ordinary law-abiding citizen cannot sing in church, in a segregated and sanitised environment. Weddings and funerals are limited as to the numbers that can attend. Restaurants and pubs remain closed; yet thousands can march, demonstrate, shout and scream quite openly.

23rd March

People are affected in different ways by the limitations of lockdown and the ways to cope with the virus. We are allowed out on our own to exercise. Some wear masks when out walking, some do not. I find it strange that some cyclists wear masks; their choice, but it demonstrates the divergence in society when joggers run along sweating, puffing, panting, wheezing and spitting yet without a mask.

Gill suffers from macular degeneration in her left eye and goes to hospital each month for an injection in her eye. Nasty.

Today, apart from her usual routine, she was seen by a doctor who undertook more tests. Look up, look down, look left, look right. She did not realise this was not only an eye test but intelligence test. Geography is not Gill's strong suit, directions when I am driving to pastures new and she is reading the map, usually consist of 'That way' or 'Towards the shops'. I remember one particular occasion. It was when we were looking to buy our first house together. I was driving, Gill was reading the A–Z road map. We were proceeding down a road towards the sea. The sea being at the bottom of the page. "Turn right at the end," Gill instructed. This I did and travelled for some mile or so before my own geographical radar clicked in and I felt we were going the wrong way. I stopped the car and took the A–Z atlas, retraced our trip and saw that we should have turned left at the junction, not right. Think about it. Looking at a book, a road map, it is north at the top south at the bottom. When driving from north to south, right should be left and left should be right!

25ᵗʰ March

A week or so ago, we noticed the wall at the bottom of our garden was cracking and bowing. I went online to find a builder and onto Checkatrade. Feedback I am getting is that some builders are busy until May, June or even October. I had an appointment arranged for 9.45 this morning. At just before 9.00, the front door bell rang. The builder had arrived. When asked why they were so early, it transpired they were at the wrong address! They phoned their other client to apologise, stayed, looked at our job and promised to send a quotation. We are now awaiting an 11.00 appointment. At twenty past eleven, I telephone the absent tradesperson (can't say tradesman). I was told his car was broken into last night and his paperwork stolen so he did not know my telephone number to call. I think this chap, responded to my online advert showing my telephone number, but I let that pass. I am told he is 25 minutes away. At 12.15, I call again to be told he is two minutes away. I am fed up, want to go out shopping and tell him not to bother coming. "I am only ten minutes away," says the voice on the phone. I said to him that his first estimates were that he was two minutes away, now he is telling me he is just ten minutes away; perhaps he is going the wrong way so don't bother to turn up. I hung up and went shopping. We are rather short of wine. It seems builders who are any good, are very, very busy; those who can't tell the time leave me to wonder what the quality of their work is going to be.

4th April

It is Gill's birthday tomorrow. Due to lockdown, there will be no party; there will be no meal at a restaurant; there will be no theatre or cinema treat, no pub lunch. So, I said as a special something for her birthday she could defrost the freezer.

6th April

I received a telephone call this morning from a company I telephoned on or about 20th March to come and price up the repair/replacement of my fence. There was originally no answer from the company, and I had left an answerphone message. Despite getting their details from the local

Checkatrade brochure, he told me, I lived too far away and they didn't travel that far.

8th April

This morning, Gill had a satsuma with her breakfast. She had twelve pips in it. Can you imagine a fruit so small having twelve pips? Outrageous, I think I should write to Asda and complain; there was insufficient fruit in their satsumas. I had one, and there were no pips at all. I thought that must be an omen for the day.

I have finished my last book so nothing to read, and it will be a couple of days until Amazon deliver a new batch of books. Seven for £21, which I thought was a bargain. I have read so much/many of my usual authors that I now struggle to find anything to read. I changed tack a few days ago and ordered a job lot written by an author I had not come across previously.

Having finished lunch and awaiting the final tradesman coming this afternoon to quote for the garden wall repair/renewal, I am bored. Gill is on her computer on some game or other. I asked if there was any washing, polishing, hoovering, ironing, dusting, weeding or painting she could be doing rather than just sitting down…Apparently, not.

I have an appointment this afternoon from a fencing company. They are scheduled to be here between 2.00–3.00 pm. At 3.20, I telephoned the company to be met with a recorded answerphone from a business line. A business telephone line! It does make me so frustrated how people run their business. I left a polite message. Some fifteen minutes later, I received a call from the company. The guy on the phone was obviously in his car travelling and said he had received a missed call from me. Having explained who I was and that I had been expecting him earlier in the afternoon, he excused himself by saying he had had car trouble. Does 'car trouble' excuse or explain why he could not telephone customers with whom he has a business appointment to say he was running late? Any reasonable person will accept 'things happen'. It does wind me up when tradespersons act so inconsiderately and then expect you to employ them with thousands of pounds worth of work. How can you trust someone who is so inconsiderate or can't tell the time?

10ᵗʰ April

I saw on a television advert last night an advert for SURE Advanced Deodorant that offered 72-hour protection. They seemed very keen and eager to emphasise that their product offered far longer protection than other 'leading brands'. I don't think I would want to be associated with a customer base that thought being unwashed for three days was a good thing. Why would you want 72-hour protection against smelly armpits? For goodness' sake, wash and make do with whatever product you choose.

12ᵗʰ April

Lockdown starts to unwind as of today. Non-essential shops can open; restaurants and pubs can serve customers but outside only. We took the opportunity to go to the Lamb in Rustington. There were about thirty people in the garden. It was great to be back in a social environment. We enjoyed a well-sanitised, well-segregated experience, a nice lunch and went home happy.

13th April

I went into Bognor today to try and get a haircut. Fully booked. I made an appointment to return on Thursday.

We decided to go to the Vardar Restaurant for lunch. Another outside experience, but why not? We have not been able to go to a restaurant for several months and you never know when 'Big Brother' will put us back into lockdown again. We sat in a heated cabin in the well-manicured garden and enjoyed another very nice lunch.

The grass in our rear garden has large areas of moss and looks rubbish. We have had a 'man what does' in to do some magic. Apparently, magic does not work on gardens; hard work seems to be the answer. We drove to the garden centre to buy some top soil and grass seed. We were disappointed, amazed but not surprised to see the A259 road works clogging up all traffic. Road side trees have been culled, grass verges have disappeared while traffic cones and barriers are strategically placed to achieve the greatest annoyance to road traffic. At mid-afternoon on a sunny afternoon in April, where are all the workmen? Not a single workman to be seen in miles of road works. Are the road works to the benefit of motorists? No, the council are putting in yet another bicycle lane at the cost of millions of pounds to the benefit of maybe three bicyclists an hour. As for the workmen, whenever we struggle through this stretch of road it is always jammed and never does one see a workman. I suppose the mantra to people working on behalf of local authorities is 'Why do in three months what you can spin out and get paid for over three years.'

19th April

It is that time of year when I aim to kit out the garden, plant out those plants that have been kept indoors over winter and buy some bedding plants to fill out the various spaces. We went to three garden centres along the A259. True to form, at 9.20 on a sunny April Monday morning, not a workman in sight. Steel barriers remain in place, orange and white cones to squeeze traffic into a single lane yet not one person was working.

22nd April

I read in the newspaper today it cost councils £250 million to clean up after fly-tippers. Why don't they re-open local municipal tips and let people dump their rubbish for free as we used to do up until last month? We now have to make an appointment to go to the tip. That is why people are more likely to fly tip, because the dumps are closed. This makes no sense at all.

Libraries and book shops have now re-opened. I would not be at all surprised to see that the politics section has been removed to the comic book section. It beggar's belief that some people who are elected to public office have so little common sense.

23rd April

Yet another warm, bright and sunny day. I am sure we will soon be told this April has been one of the driest and warmest

Aprils on record. It has been lovely. Gill and I decided to go for a walk around Swanbourne Lake in Arundel. Arundel was very crowded. I think there was a flower festival on at the castle. It was difficult to park. We decided as we could not find a parking space we would have an early lunch at the Black Rabbit. We drove on to the pub and found that was also crowded with people queuing. It is of course all outside seating, and we saw no vacant tables so we turned around and went back the way we came. On our way back, we saw a car pull out from a parking space, drove in and parked. We went for our delayed walk around the lake.

25ᵗʰ April

The grass in the back garden was recently treated for moss and weeds. There are now several black and brown patches. I went to Wicks this morning to buy some grass seed. It was not too busy, but when I found the queue to pay, it wound around the aisles and was about 30 deep. There were three checkout desks operating so it only took about ten minutes to reach the front.

"Can I help you?"

"A large black Americano coffee please."

"Sorry!"

"A large black Americano coffee please. This is the queue for refreshments, isn't it?"

Very dumb, blank look. Obviously not having one of her better days. Or maybe she thought I was mad!

We enjoy quiz shows on television and there are often Celebrity shows where 'D' list celebrities play for charity. Tonight, on a celebrity edition of The Chase, the puppet Basil

Brush was the most famous of the celebrities! That speaks volumes of the quality of celebs invited, or my lack of modern-day entertainment knowledge.